SELECTED POEMS
Margaret Atwood

Toronto Oxford University Press 1976

Grateful acknowledgement is made to the House of Anansi for permission to include poems from *The Circle Game* and *Power Politics.*

Poems from *The Animals in That Country, Procedures for Underground,* and *The Journals of Susanna Moodie* © Oxford University Press, Canadian Branch. Poems from *You Are Happy* © Margaret Atwood.

Selection © Margaret Atwood.

ISBN 19-5402510

1 2 3 4 — 9 8 7 6

Printed in Canada by John Deyell Limited

Contents

Contents

From PROCEDURES FOR UNDERGROUND

From POWER POLITICS

Contents

From

The Circle Game

1966

THIS IS A PHOTOGRAPH OF ME

It was taken some time ago.
At first it seems to be
a smeared
print: blurred lines and grey flecks
blended with the paper;

then, as you scan
it, you see in the left-hand corner
a thing that is like a branch: part of a tree
(balsam or spruce) emerging
and, to the right, halfway up
what ought to be a gentle
slope, a small frame house.

In the background there is a lake,
and beyond that, some low hills.

(The photograph was taken
the day after I drowned.

I am in the lake, in the center
of the picture, just under the surface.

It is difficult to say where
precisely, or to say
how large or small I am:
the effect of water
on light is a distortion

but if you look long enough,
eventually
you will be able to see me.)

AFTER THE FLOOD, WE

We must be the only ones
left, in the mist that has risen
everywhere as well
as in these woods

I walk across the bridge
towards the safety of high ground
(the tops of the trees are like islands)

gathering the sunken
bones of the drowned mothers
(hard and round in my hands)
while the white mist washes
around my legs like water;

fish must be swimming
down in the forest beneath us,
like birds, from tree to tree
and a mile away
the city, wide and silent,
is lying lost, far undersea.

You saunter beside me, talking
of the beauty of the morning,
not even knowing
that there has been a flood,

tossing small pebbles
at random over your shoulder
into the deep thick air,

not hearing the first stumbling
footsteps of the almost-born
coming (slowly) behind us,
not seeing
the almost-human
brutal faces forming
(slowly)
out of stone.

THE CITY PLANNERS

Cruising these residential Sunday
streets in dry August sunlight:
what offends us is
the sanities:
the houses in pedantic rows, the planted
sanitary trees, assert
levelness of surface like a rebuke
to the dent in our car door.
No shouting here, or
shatter of glass; nothing more abrupt
than the rational whine of a power mower
cutting a straight swath in the discouraged grass.

But though the driveways neatly
sidestep hysteria
by being even, the roofs all display
the same slant of avoidance to the hot sky,
certain things:
the smell of spilled oil a faint

sickness lingering in the garages,
a splash of paint on brick surprising as a bruise,
a plastic hose poised in a vicious
coil; even the too-fixed stare of the wide windows

give momentary access to
the landscape behind or under
the future cracks in the plaster

when the houses, capsized, will slide
obliquely into the clay seas, gradual as glaciers
that right now nobody notices.

That is where the City Planners
with the insane faces of political conspirators
are scattered over unsurveyed
territories, concealed from each other,
each in his own private blizzard;

guessing directions, they sketch
transitory lines rigid as wooden borders
on a wall in the white vanishing air

tracing the panic of suburb
order in a bland madness of snows.

EVENTUAL PROTEUS

I held you
through all your shifts
of structure: while your bones turned
from caved rock back to marrow,
the dangerous
fur faded to hair
the bird's cry died in your throat
the treebark paled from your skin
the leaves from your eyes

till you limped back again
to daily man:
a lounger on streetcorners
in iron-shiny gabardine
a leaner on stale tables;
at night a twitching sleeper
dreaming of crumbs and rinds and a sagging woman
caged by a sour bed.

The early
languages are obsolete.

These days we keep
our weary distances:
sparring in the vacant spaces
of peeling rooms
and rented minutes, climbing
all the expected stairs, our voices
abraded with fatigue,
our bodies wary.

Shrunk by my disbelief
you cannot raise
the green gigantic skies, resume
the legends of your disguises:
this shape is final.

Now, when you come near
attempting towards me across
these sheer cavernous
inches of air

your flesh has no more stories
or surprises;

my face flinches
under the sarcastic
tongues of your estranging
fingers,
the caustic remark of your kiss.

THE CIRCLE GAME

i

The children on the lawn
joined hand to hand
go round and round

each arm going into
the next arm, around
full circle
until it comes
back into each of the single
bodies again

They are singing, but
not to each other:
their feet move
almost in time to the singing

We can see
the concentration on
their faces, their eyes
fixed on the empty
moving spaces just in
front of them.

We might mistake this
tranced moving for joy
but there is no joy in it

We can see (arm in arm)
as we watch them go
round and round
intent, almost
studious (the grass

underfoot ignored, the trees
circling the lawn
ignored, the lake ignored)
that the whole point
for them
of going round and round
is (faster
        slower)
going round and round

ii

Being with you
here, in this room

is like groping through a mirror
whose glass has melted
to the consistency
of gelatin

You refuse to be
(and I)
an exact reflection, yet
will not walk from the glass,
be separate.

Anyway, it is right
that they have put
so many mirrors here
(chipped, hung crooked)
in this room with its high transom
and empty wardrobe; even
the back of the door
has one.

There are people in the next room
arguing, opening and closing drawers
(the walls are thin)

You look past me, listening
to them, perhaps, or
watching
your own reflection somewhere
behind my head,
over my shoulder

You shift, and the bed
sags under us, losing its focus

there is someone in the next room

there is always

(your face
remote, listening)

someone in the next room.

iii

However,
in all their games
there seems
to be some reason

however
abstract they
at first appear

When we read them legends
in the evening
of monstrous battles, and secret
betrayals in the forest
and brutal deaths,

they scarcely listened;
one yawned and fidgeted; another
chewed the wooden handle
of a hammer;
the youngest one examined
a slight cut on his toe,

and we wondered how
they could remain
completely without fear
or even interest
as the final sword slid through
the dying hero.

The next night
walking along the beach

we found the trenches
they had been making:
fortified with pointed sticks
driven into the sides
of their sand moats

and a lake-enclosed island
with no bridges:

a last attempt
(however
eroded by the water
in an hour)

to make
maybe, a refuge human
and secure from the reach

of whatever walks along
(sword hearted)
these night beaches.

iv

Returning to the room:
I notice how
all your word-
plays, calculated ploys
of the body, the witticisms
of touch, are now
attempts to keep me
at a certain distance
and (at length) avoid
admitting I am here

I watch you
watching my face
indifferently
yet with the same taut curiosity
with which you might regard
a suddenly discovered part
of your own body:
a wart perhaps,

and I remember that
you said
in childhood you were
a tracer of maps
(not making but) moving
a pen or a forefinger

over the courses of the rivers,
the different colours
that mark the rise of mountains;
a memorizer
of names (to hold
these places
in their proper places)

So now you trace me
like a country's boundary
or a strange new wrinkle in
your own wellknown skin
and I am fixed, stuck
down on the outspread map
of this room, of your mind's continent
   (here and yet not here, like
   the wardrobe and the mirrors
   the voices through the wall
   your body ignored on the bed),

transfixed
by your eyes'
cold blue thumbtacks

v

The children like the block
of grey stone that was once a fort
but now is a museum:

especially
they like the guns
and the armour brought from
other times and countries

and when they go home
their drawings will be full
for some days, of swords
archaic sunburst maces
broken spears
and vivid red explosions.

While they explore
the cannons
(they aren't our children)

we walk outside along
the earthworks, noting
how they are crumbling
under the unceasing
attacks of feet and flower roots;

The weapons
that were once outside
sharpening themselves on war
are now indoors
there, in the fortress,
fragile
in glass cases;

Why is it
(I'm thinking
of the careful moulding
round the stonework archways)
that in this time, such
elaborate defences keep
things that are no longer
(much)
worth defending?

vi

And you play the safe game
the orphan game

the ragged winter game
that says, I am alone

(hungry: I know you want me
to play it also)

the game of the waif who stands
at every picture window,

shivering, pinched nose pressed
against the glass, the snow
collecting on his neck,
watching the happy families

(a game of envy)

Yet he despises them: they are so
Victorian Christmas-card:
the cheap paper shows
under the pigments of
their cheerful fire-
places and satin-
ribboned suburban laughter
and they have their own forms
of parlour
games: father and mother
playing father and mother

He's glad
to be left
out by himself
in the cold

(hugging himself).

When I tell you this,
you say (with a smile fake
as a tinsel icicle):

You do it too.

Which in some ways
is a lie, but also I suppose
is right, as usual:

although I tend to pose
in other seasons
outside other windows.

vii

Summer again;
in the mirrors of this room
the children wheel, singing
the same song;

This casual bed
scruffy as dry turf,
the counterpane
rumpled with small burrows, is
their grassy lawn

and these scuffed walls
contain their circling trees,
that low clogged sink
their lake

(a wasp comes,
drawn by the piece of sandwich
left on the nearby beach
        (how carefully you do
        such details);
one of the children flinches
but won't let go)

You make them
turn and turn, according to
the closed rules of your games,
but there is no joy in it

and as we lie
arm in arm, neither
joined nor separate
        (your observations change me
        to a spineless woman in
        a cage of bones, obsolete fort
        pulled inside out),
our lips moving
almost in time to their singing,

listening to the opening
and closing of the drawers
in the next room

(of course there is always
danger but where
would you locate it)

(the children spin
a round cage of glass
from the warm air
with their thread-thin
insect voices)

and as we lie
here, caught
in the monotony of wandering
from room to room, shifting
the place of our defences,

I want to break
these bones, your prisoning rhythms
        (winter,
            summer)
all the glass cases,

erase all maps,
crack the protecting
eggshell of your turning
singing children:

I want the circle
broken.

MIGRATION: C.P.R.

i

Escaping from allegories
in the misty east, where inherited events
barnacle on the mind; where every gloved handshake
might be a finger pointing; you can't look
in store windows without seeing
reflections/ remnants of privateer
bones or methodist grandfathers with jaws
carved as wood pulpits warning
of the old evil; where not-quite-
forgotten histories
make the boards of lineal frame
farmhouses rotten

the fishermen
sit all day on old wharves facing
neither sea-
wards nor inland, mending
and untangling their old nets
of thought

and language is the law

we ran west

wanting
a place of absolute
unformed beginning

(the train
an ark
upheld on the brain's darkness)

but the inner lakes reminded
us too much of ancient oceans
first flood: blood-
enemy and substance
(was our train like
an ark or like a seasnake?

and the prairies were so nearly
empty as prehistory
that each of the
few solid objects took some great
implication, hidden but
more sudden than a signpost

(like an inscribed shard, broken bowl
dug at a desert level
where they thought
no man had been,
or a burned bone)

(every dwarf tree portentous
with twisted wisdom, though
we knew no
apples grew there

and that shape, gazing
at nothing
by a hooftrampled streamside:
it could
have been a centaur)

and even the mountains
at the approach, were
conical, iconic
again:

(tents
in the desert?   triangular
ships?   towers?   breasts?
words)
again
these barriers

ii

Once in the pass, the steep
faulted gorges were at last
real: we
tossed our eastern
suitcases from the caboose
and all our baggage
overboard
left in our wake
along the tracks
and (we saw) our train became
only a train, in real
danger of falling; strained
speechless through those new mountains
we stepped
unbound
into

what a free emerging
on the raw
streets and hills
without meaning
always creeping up behind us
(that cold touch on the shoulder)

our faces scraped as blank
as we could wish them

(but needing new
houses, new
dishes, new
husks)

iii

There are more secondhand
stores here than we expected:
though we brought nothing with us
(we thought)
we have begun to unpack.

A residual brass bedstead
scratched with the initials
of generic brides and grooms;
chipped squat teapots: old totemic
mothers; a boxful
of used hats.

In the forest, even
apart from the trodden
paths, we can tell (from the sawn
firstumps) that many
have passed the same way
some time before
this (hieroglyphics
carved in the bark)

Things here grow from the ground
too insistently
green to seem
spontaneous. (My skeletons, I think,
will be still
in the windows when I look,
as well as the books

and the index-
fingered gloves.)

There is also a sea
that refuses to stay in the harbour:
becomes opaque
air or throws
brown seaweeds like small drowned hands
up on these shores

(the fishermen
are casting their nets here
as well)
and blunted mountains
rolling
      (the first whales maybe?)
in the
inescapable mists.

JOURNEY TO THE INTERIOR

There are similarities
I notice: that the hills
which the eyes make flat as a wall, welded
together, open as I move
to let me through; become
endless as prairies; that the trees
grow spindly, have their roots
often in swamps; that this is a poor country;
that a cliff is not known
as rough except by hand, and is
therefore inaccessible. Mostly
that travel is not the easy going

from point to point, a dotted
line on a map, location
plotted on a square surface
but that I move surrounded by a tangle
of branches, a net of air and alternate
light and dark, at all times;
that there are no destinations
apart from this.

There are differences
of course: the lack of reliable charts;
more important, the distraction of small details:
your shoe among the brambles under the chair
where it shouldn't be; lucent
white mushrooms and a paring knife
on the kitchen table; a sentence
crossing my path, sodden as a fallen log
I'm sure I passed yesterday

                     (have I been
walking in circles again?)

but mostly the danger:
many have been here, but only
some have returned safely.

A compass is useless; also
trying to take directions
from the movements of the sun,
which are erratic;
and words here are as pointless
as calling in a vacant
wilderness.
             Whatever I do I must
keep my head. I know
it is easier for me to lose my way
forever here, than in other landscapes

SOME OBJECTS OF WOOD AND STONE

i   Totems

We went to the park
where they kept the wooden people:
static, multiple
uprooted and trans-
planted.

Their faces were restored,
freshly-painted.
In front of them
the other wooden people
posed for each others' cameras
and nearby a new booth
sold replicas and souvenirs.

One of the people was real.
It lay on its back, smashed
by a toppling fall or just
the enduring of minor winters.
Only one of the heads had
survived intact, and it was
also beginning to decay
but there was a
life in the progressing
of old wood back to
the earth, obliteration

that the clear-hewn
standing figures lacked.

As for us, perennial watchers,
tourists of another kind
there is nothing for us to worship;
no pictures of ourselves, no blue-
sky summer fetishes, no postcards
we can either buy, or
smiling
be.

There are few totems that remain
living for us.
Though in passing,
through glass we notice

dead trees in the seared meadows
dead roots bleaching in the swamps.

ii   Pebbles

Talking was difficult. Instead
we gathered coloured pebbles
from the places on the beach
where they occurred.

They were sea-smoothed, sea-completed.
They enclosed what they intended
to mean in shapes
as random and necessary
as the shapes of words

and when finally
we spoke
the sounds of our voices fell
into the air   single and

solid and rounded and really
there
and then dulled, and then like sounds
gone,   a fistful of gathered
pebbles there was no point
in taking home, dropped on a beachful
of other coloured pebbles

and when we turned to go
a flock of small
birds flew scattered by the
fright of our sudden moving
and disappeared: hard

sea pebbles
thrown solid for an instant
against the sky

flight of words

iii   Carved Animals

The small carved
animal is passed from
hand to hand
around the circle
until the stone grows warm

touching, the hands do not know
the form of animal
which was made or
the true form of stone
uncovered

and the hands, the fingers the
hidden small bones
of the hands bend to hold the shape,
shape themselves, grow
cold with the stone's cold, grow
also animal, exchange
until the skin wonders
if stone is human

In the darkness later
and even when the animal
has gone, they keep
the image of that
inner shape

hands holding warm
hands holding
the half-formed air

PRE-AMPHIBIAN

Again so I subside
nudged by the softening
driftwood of your body,
tangle on you like a water-
weed caught
on a submerged treelimb

with sleep like a swamp
growing, closing around me
sending its tendrils through the brown
sediments of darkness
where we   transmuted   are
part of this warm rotting
of vegetable flesh
this quiet spawning of roots

released
from the lucidities of day
when you are something I can
trace a line around, with eyes
cut shapes
from air, the element
where we
must calculate according to
solidities

but here I blur
into you   our breathing sinking
to green milleniums
and   sluggish   in our blood
all ancestors
are warm fish moving

The earth
shifts, bringing
the moment before focus, when
these tides recede; and we
see each other through the
hardening scales of waking

stranded, astounded
in a drying world

we flounder, the air
ungainly in our new lungs
with sunlight steaming merciless on the shores of morning

AGAINST STILL LIFE

Orange in the middle of a table:

It isn't enough
to walk around it
at a distance, saying
it's an orange:
nothing to do
with us, nothing
else: leave it alone

I want to pick it up
in my hand
I want to peel the
skin off; I want
more to be said to me
than just Orange:
want to be told
everything it has to say

And you, sitting across
the table, at a distance, with
your smile contained, and like the orange
in the sun: silent:

Your silence
isn't enough for me
now, no matter with what
contentment you fold
your hands together; I want
anything you can say
in the sunlight:

stories of your various
childhoods, aimless journeyings,
your loves; your articulate
skeleton; your posturings; your lies.

These orange silences
(sunlight and hidden smile)
make me want to
wrench you into saying;
now I'd crack your skull
like a walnut, split it like a pumpkin
to make you talk, or get
a look inside

But quietly:
if I take the orange
with care enough and hold it
gently

I may find
an egg
a sun
an orange moon
perhaps a skull; center
of all energy
resting in my hand

can change it to
whatever I desire
it to be

and you, man, orange afternoon
lover, wherever
you sit across from me
(tables, trains, buses)

if I watch
quietly enough
and long enough

at last, you will say
(maybe without speaking)

(there are mountains
inside your skull
garden and chaos, ocean
and hurricane; certain
corners of rooms, portraits
of great-grandmothers, curtains
of a particular shade;
your deserts; your private
dinosaurs; the first
woman)

all I need to know:
tell me
everything
just as it was
from the beginning.

A PLACE: FRAGMENTS

i

Here on the rim, cringing
under the cracked whip of winter
we live
in houses of ice,
but not because we want to:
in order to survive
we make what we can and have to
with what we have.

ii

Old woman I visited once
out of my way
in a little-visited province:

she had a neat
house, a clean parlour
though obsolete and poor:

a cushion with a fringe;
glass animals arranged
across the mantlepiece (a swan, a horse,
a bull); a mirror;
a teacup sent from Scotland;
several heraldic spoons;
a lamp; and in the center
of the table, a paperweight:
hollow glass globe
filled with water, and
a house, a man, a snowstorm.

The room was as
dustless as possible
and free of spiders.
                                        I
stood in the door-
way, at the fulcrum where

this trivial but
stringent inner order
held its delicate balance
with the random scattering or
clogged merging of
things: ditch by the road; dried
reeds in the wind; flat
wet bush, grey sky
sweeping away outside.

iii

The cities are only outposts.

Watch that man
walking on cement as though on snowshoes:
senses the road
a muskeg, loose mat of roots and brown
vegetable decay
or crust of ice that
easily might break and
slush or water under
suck him down

The land flows like a
sluggish current.

The mountains eddy slowly towards the sea.

iv

The people who come here also
flow: their bodies becoming
nebulous, diffused, quietly
spreading out into the air across
these interstellar sidewalks

v

This is what it must be
like in outer space
where the stars are pasted flat
against the total
black of the expanding
eye, fly-
specks of burning dust

vi

There is no center;
the centers
travel with us unseen
like our shadows
on a day when there is no sun.

We must move back:
there are too many foregrounds.

Now, clutter of twigs
across our eyes, tatter
of birds at the eye's edge; the straggle
of dead treetrunks; patch
of lichen

and in love, tangle
of limbs and fingers, the texture
of pores and lines on the skin.

vii

An other sense tugs at us:
we have lost something,
some key to these things
which must be writings
and are locked against us
or perhaps (like a potential
mine, unknown vein
of metal in the rock)
something not lost or hidden
but just not found yet

that informs, holds together
this confusion, this largeness
and dissolving:

not above or behind
or within it, but one
with it: an

identity:
something too huge and simple
for us to see.

THE EXPLORERS

The explorers will come
in several minutes
and find this island.

(It is a stunted island,
rocky, with room
for only a few trees, a thin
layer of soil; hardly
bigger than a bed.
That is how
they've missed it
until now)

Already their boats draw near,
their flags flutter,
their oars push at the water.

They will be jubilant
and shout, at finding
that there was something
they had not found before,

although this island will afford
not much more than a foothold:
little to explore;

but they will be surprised

(we can't see them yet;
we know they must be
coming, because they always come
several minutes too late)

(they won't be able
to tell how long
we were cast away, or why,
or, from these
gnawed bones,
which was the survivor)

at the two skeletons

THE SETTLERS

A second after
the first boat touched the shore,
there was a quick skirmish
brief as a twinge
and then the land was settled

(of course there was really
no shore: the water turned
to land by having
objects in it: caught and kept
from surge, made
less than immense
by networks of
roads and grids of fences)

and as for us, who drifted
picked by the sharks
during so many bluegreen

centuries before they came:
they found us
inland, stranded
on a ridge of bedrock,
defining our own island.

From our inarticulate
skeleton (so
intermixed, one
carcass),
they postulated wolves.

They dug us down
into the solid granite
where our bones grew flesh again,
came up trees and
grass.

Still
we are the salt
seas that uphold these lands.

Now horses graze
inside this fence of ribs, and

children run, with green
smiles, (not knowing
where) across
the fields of our open hands.

From

The Animals
in That Country

1968

THE ANIMALS IN THAT COUNTRY

In that country the animals
have the faces of people:

the ceremonial
cats possessing the streets

the fox run
politely to earth, the huntsmen
standing around him, fixed
in their tapestry of manners

the bull, embroidered
with blood and given
an elegant death, trumpets, his name
stamped on him, heraldic brand
because

(when he rolled
on the sand, sword in his heart, the teeth
in his blue mouth were human)

he is really a man

even the wolves, holding resonant
conversations in their
forests thickened with legend.

In this country the animals
have the faces of
animals.

Their eyes
flash once in car headlights
and are gone.

Their deaths are not elegant.

They have the faces of
no-one.

A FOUNDLING

He left himself on my doorstep,
abandoned in the shabby
basket of his own ribs.

My heart wept custard:
I took him in.

Warmed in the kitchen,
he swelled, absorbing.
He will not leave,
I am afraid to move him.

What should I feed him?

He never talks. He sits
in the middle of the kitchen floor
staring at the bright scars
traced on his body, fascinated.

At first
I thought that they were notched
on him by pain

but now I see
that they are only the coloured pictures
of places he once
lived, and thinks
that no-one else has ever been.

THE LANDLADY

This is the lair of the landlady.

She is
a raw voice
loose in the rooms beneath me,

the continuous henyard
squabble going on below
thought in this house like
the bicker of blood through the head.

She is everywhere, intrusive as the smells
that bulge in under my doorsill;
she presides over my
meagre eating, generates
the light for eyestrain.

From her I rent my time:
she slams
my days like doors.
Nothing is mine

and when I dream images
of daring escapes through the snow
I find myself walking
always over a vast face
which is the land-
lady's, and wake up shouting.

She is a bulk, a knot
swollen in space. Though I have tried
to find some way around
her, my senses
are cluttered by perception
and can't see through her.

She stands there, a raucous fact
blocking my way:
immutable, a slab
of what is real,

solid as bacon.

A FORTIFICATION

Upon waking a nerve complains in the
(briefly) voice of an airdrill
because my opening eyes close hydraulic
doors between the hands and some other time

that can't exist, my control panel
whispers softly as a diamond
cutting glass. I get up, extend the feet
into my body which is a metal spacesuit.

I have armed myself, yes I am safe: safe:
the grass can't hurt me.
My senses swivel like guns in their fixed sockets:
I am barriered from leaves and blood.

But there is a thing, person, a blunt groping
though the light denies it: what face
could be here among the lamps and the clear edges?
Still for an instant I

catch sight of the other creature,
the one that has real skin, real hair,
vanishing down the line of cells
back to the lost forest of being vulnerable

AT THE TOURIST CENTRE IN BOSTON

There is my country under glass,
a white relief-
map with red dots for the cities,
reduced to the size of a wall

and beside it 10 blownup snapshots
one for each province,
in purple-browns and odd reds,
the green of the trees dulled;
all blues however
of an assertive purity.

Mountains and lakes and more lakes
(though Quebec is a restaurant and Ontario the empty
interior of the parliament buildings),
with nobody climbing the trails and hauling out
the fish and splashing in the water

but arrangements of grinning tourists—
look here, Saskatchewan
is a flat lake, some convenient rocks
where two children pose with a father
and the mother is cooking something
in immaculate slacks by a smokeless fire,
her teeth white as detergent.

Whose dream is this, I would like to know:
is this a manufactured
hallucination, a cynical fiction, a lure
for export only?

I seem to remember people,
at least in the cities, also slush,
machines and assorted garbage. Perhaps
that was my private mirage

which will just evaporate
when I go back. Or the citizens will be gone,
run off to the peculiarly-
green forests
to wait among the brownish mountains
for the platoons of tourists
and plan their odd red massacres.

Unsuspecting
window lady, I ask you:

Do you see nothing
watching you from under the water?

Was the sky ever that blue?

Who really lives there?

ELEGY FOR THE GIANT TORTOISES

Let others pray for the passenger pigeon
the dodo, the whooping crane, the eskimo:
everyone must specialize

I will confine myself to a meditation
upon the giant tortoises
withering finally on a remote island.

I concentrate in subway stations,
in parks, I can't quite see them,
they move to the peripheries of my eyes

but on the last day they will be there;
already the event
like a wave travelling shapes vision:

on the road where I stand they will materialize,
plodding past me in a straggling line
awkward without water

their small heads pondering
from side to side, their useless armour
sadder than tanks and history,

in their closed gaze ocean and sunlight paralysed,
lumbering up the steps, under the archways
toward the square glass altars

where the brittle gods are kept,
the relics of what we have destroyed,
our holy and obsolete symbols.

ROOMINGHOUSE, WINTER

Catprints, dogprints, marks
of ancient children
have made the paths we follow

to the vestibule, piled
with overshoes, ownerless letters
a wooden sled.

The threadbare treads
on the stairs. The trails
worn by alien feet

in time through the forest snowdrifts
of the corridor to this remnant, this
discarded door

What disturbs me in the bathroom
is the unclaimed toothbrush.

In the room itself, none
of the furniture is mine.

The plates are on the table
to weight it down.

I call you sometimes
To make sure you are still there.

Tomorrow, when you come to dinner
They will tell you I never lived here.

My window is a funnel
for the shapes of chaos

      In the backyard, frozen bones, the childrens'
      voices, derelict
      objects

Inside, the wall
buckles; the pressure

balanced by this clear
small silence.

We must resist. We must refuse
to disappear

I said, In exile
survival
is the first necessity.

After that (I say this
tentatively)
we might begin

Survive what?   you said.

In the weak light you looked
over your shoulder.
               You said

Nobody ever survives.

IT IS DANGEROUS TO READ NEWSPAPERS

While I was building neat
castles in the sandbox,
the hasty pits were
filling with bulldozed corpses

and as I walked to the school
washed and combed, my feet
stepping on the cracks in the cement
detonated red bombs.

Now I am grownup
and literate, and I sit in my chair
as quietly as a fuse

and the jungles are flaming, the under-
brush is charged with soldiers,
the names on the difficult
maps go up in smoke.

I am the cause, I am a stockpile of chemical
toys, my body
is a deadly gadget,
I reach out in love, my hands are guns,
my good intentions are completely lethal.

Even my
passive eyes transmute
everything I look at to the pocked
black and white of a war photo,
how
can I stop myself

It is dangerous to read newspapers.

Each time I hit a key
on my electric typewriter,
speaking of peaceful trees

another village explodes.

PROGRESSIVE INSANITIES OF A PIONEER

i

He stood, a point
on a sheet of green paper
proclaiming himself the centre,

with no walls, no borders
anywhere; the sky no height
above him, totally un-
enclosed
and shouted:

Let me out!

ii

He dug the soil in rows,
imposed himself with shovels
He asserted
into the furrows, I
am not random.

The ground
replied with aphorisms:

a tree-sprout, a nameless
weed, words
he couldn't understand.

iii

The house pitched
the plot staked
in the middle of nowhere.

At night the mind
inside, in the middle
of nowhere.

The idea of an animal
patters across the roof.

In the darkness the fields
defend themselves with fences
in vain:
        everything
        is getting in.

iv

By daylight he resisted.
He said, disgusted
with the swamp's clamourings and the outbursts
of rocks,
        This is not order
        but the absence
        of order.

He was wrong, the unanswering
forest implied:

It was
an ordered absence

v

For many years
he fished for a great vision,
dangling the hooks of sown
roots under the surface
of the shallow earth.

It was like
enticing whales with a bent
pin. Besides he thought

in that country
only the worms were biting.

vi

If he had known unstructured
space is a deluge
and stocked his log house-
boat with all the animals

even the wolves,

he might have floated.

But obstinate he
stated, The land is solid
and stamped,

watching his foot sink
down through stone
up to the knee.

vii

Things
refused to name themselves; refused
to let him name them.

The wolves hunted
outside.

On his beaches, his clearings,
by the surf of under-
growth breaking
at his feet, he foresaw
disintegration
                    and in the end
through eyes
made ragged by his
effort, the tension
between subject and object,

the green
vision, the unnamed
whale invaded.

SPEECHES FOR DR FRANKENSTEIN

i

I, the performer
in the tense arena, glittered
under the fluorescent moon. Was bent
masked by the table. Saw what focused
my intent: the emptiness

The air filled with an ether of cheers.

My wrist extended a scalpel.

ii

The table is a flat void,
barren as total freedom. Though behold

A sharp twist
like taking a jar top off

and it is a living
skeleton, mine, round,
that lies on the plate before me

red as a pomegranate,
every cell a hot light.

iii

I circle, confront
my opponent. The thing

refuses to be shaped, it moves
like yeast. I thrust,

the thing fights back.
It dissolves, growls, grows crude claws;

The air is dusty with blood.

It springs. I cut
with delicate precision.

The specimens
ranged on the shelves, applaud.

The thing falls Thud. A cat
anatomized.

O secret
form of the heart, now I have you.

iv

Now I shall ornament you.
What would you like?

Baroque scrolls on your ankles?
A silver navel?

I am the universal weaver;
I have eight fingers.

I complicate you;
I surround you with intricate ropes.

What web shall I wrap you in?
Gradually I pin you down.

What equation shall
I carve and seal in your skull?

What size will I make you?
Where should I put your eyes?

v

I was insane with skill:
I made you perfect.

I should have chosen instead
to curl you small as a seed,

trusted beginnings. Now I wince
before this plateful of results:

core and rind, the flesh between
already turning rotten.

I stand in the presence
of the destroyed god:

a rubble of tendons,
knuckles and raw sinews.

Knowing that the work is mine
how can I love you?

These archives of potential
time exude fear like a smell.

vi

You arise, larval
and shrouded in the flesh I gave you;

I, who have no covering
left but a white cloth skin

escape from you. You are red,
you are human and distorted.

You have been starved,
you are hungry. I have nothing to feed you.

I pull around me, running,
a cape of rain.

What was my ravenous motive?
Why did I make you?

vii

Reflection, you have stolen
everything you needed:

my joy, my ability
to suffer.

You have transmuted
yourself to me: I am
a vestige, I am numb.

Now you accuse me of murder.

Can't you see
I am incapable?

Blood of my brain,
it is you who have killed these people.

viii

Since I dared
to attempt impious wonders

I must pursue
that animal I once denied
was mine.

Over this vacant winter
plain, the sky is a black shell;
I move within it, a cold
kernel of pain.

I scratch huge rescue messages
on the solid
snow; in vain. My heart's
husk is a stomach. I am its food.

ix

The sparkling monster
gambols there ahead,
his mane electric:
This is his true place.

He dances in spirals on the ice,
his clawed feet
kindling shaggy fires.

His happiness
is now the chase itself:
he traces it in light,
his paths contain it.

I am the gaunt hunter
necessary for his patterns,
lurking, gnawing leather.

x

The creature, his arctic hackles
bristling, spreads
over the dark ceiling,
his paws on the horizons,
rolling the world like a snowball.

He glows and says:

Doctor, my shadow
shivering on the table,
you dangle on the leash
of your own longing;
your need grows teeth.

You sliced me loose

and said it was
Creation. I could feel the knife.
Now you would like to heal
that chasm in your side,
but I recede. I prowl.

I will not come when you call.

BACKDROP ADDRESSES COWBOY

Starspangled cowboy
sauntering out of the almost-
silly West, on your face
a porcelain grin,
tugging a papier-mâché cactus
on wheels behind you with a string,

you are innocent as a bathtub
full of bullets.

Your righteous eyes, your laconic
trigger-fingers
people the streets with villains:
as you move, the air in front of you
blossoms with targets

and you leave behind you a heroic
trail of desolation:
beer bottles
slaughtered by the side
of the road, bird-
skulls bleaching in the sunset.

I ought to be watching
from behind a cliff or a cardboard storefront
when the shooting starts, hands clasped
in admiration,

but I am elsewhere.

Then what about me

what about the I
confronting you on that border
you are always trying to cross?

I am the horizon
you ride towards, the thing you can never lasso

I am also what surrounds you:
my brain
scattered with your
tincans, bones, empty shells,
the litter of your invasions.

I am the space you desecrate
as you pass through.

I WAS READING A SCIENTIFIC ARTICLE

They have photographed the brain
and here is the picture, it is full of
branches as I always suspected,

each time you arrive the electricity
of seeing you is a huge
tree lumbering through my skull, the roots waving.

It is an earth, its fibres wrap
things buried, your forgotten words
are graved in my head, an intricate

red blue and pink prehensile chemistry
veined like a leaf
network, or is it a seascape
with corals and shining tentacles.

I touch you, I am created in you
somewhere as a complex
filament of light

You rest on me and my shoulder holds

your heavy unbelievable
skull, crowded with radiant
suns, a new planet, the people
submerged in you, a lost civilization
I can never excavate:

my hands trace the contours of a total
universe, its different
colours, flowers, its undiscovered
animals, violent or serene

its other air
its claws

its paradise rivers

MORE AND MORE

More and more frequently the edges
of me dissolve and I become
a wish to assimilate the world, including
you, if possible through the skin
like a cool plant's tricks with oxygen
and live by a harmless green burning.

I would not consume
you, or ever
finish, you would still be there
surrounding me, complete
as the air.

Unfortunately I don't have leaves.
Instead I have eyes
and teeth and other non-green
things which rule out osmosis.

So be careful, I mean it,
I give you a fair warning:

This kind of hunger draws
everything into its own
space; nor can we
talk it all over, have a calm
rational discussion.

There is no reason for this, only
a starved dog's logic about bones.

A VOICE

A voice from the other country
stood on the grass. He became
part of the grass.

      The sun shone
      greenly on the blades of his hands

Then we
appeared, climbing down
the hill, you
in your blue sweater.

He could see that
we did not occupy
the space, as he did. We
were merely in it

      My skirt was yellow
      small
      between his eyes

We moved along
      the grass, through
the air that was inside
his head. We did not see him.

      He could smell
      the leather on our feet

We walked
small
across
his field of vision (he
watching us) and disappeared.

His brain grew over
the places we had been.

He sat. He was curious
about himself. He wondered
how he had managed to think us.

THE REINCARNATION OF CAPTAIN COOK

Earlier than I could learn
the maps had been coloured in.
When I pleaded, the kings told me
nothing was left to explore.

I set out anyway, but
everywhere I went
there were historians, wearing
wreaths and fake teeth
belts; or in the deserts, cairns
and tourists. Even the caves had
candle stubs, inscriptions quickly
scribbled in darkness. I could

never arrive. Always
the names got there before.

Now I am old I know my
mistake was my acknowledging
of maps. The eyes raise
tired monuments.

Burn down
the atlases, I shout
to the park benches; and go

past the cenotaph
waving a blank banner
across the street, beyond
the corner

into a new land cleaned of geographies,
its beach gleaming with arrows.

AXIOM

Axiom: you are a sea.
Your eye-
lids curve over chaos

My hands
where they touch you, create
small inhabited islands

Soon you will be
all earth: a known
land, a country.

The Journals of
Susanna Moodie

1970

*I take this picture of myself
and with my sewing scissors
cut out the face.*

Now it is more accurate:

*where my eyes were,
every-
thing appears*

DISEMBARKING AT QUEBEC

Is it my clothes, my way of walking,
the things I carry in my hand
—a book, a bag with knitting—
the incongruous pink of my shawl

this space cannot hear

or is it my own lack
of conviction which makes
these vistas of desolation,
long hills, the swamps, the barren sand, the glare
of sun on the bone-white
driftlogs, omens of winter,
the moon alien in day-
time a thin refusal

The others leap, shout

                    Freedom!

The moving water will not show me
my reflection.

The rocks ignore.

I am a word
in a foreign language.

FURTHER ARRIVALS

After we had crossed the long illness
that was the ocean, we sailed up-river

On the first island
the immigrants threw off their clothes
and danced like sandflies

We left behind one by one
the cities rotting with cholera,
one by one our civilized
distinctions

and entered a large darkness.

It was our own
ignorance we entered.

I have not come out yet

My brain gropes nervous
tentacles in the night, sends out
fears hairy as bears,
demands lamps; or waiting

for my shadowy husband, hears
malice in the trees' whispers.

I need wolf's eyes to see
the truth.

I refuse to look in a mirror.

Whether the wilderness is
real or not
depends on who lives there.

FIRST NEIGHBOURS

The people I live among, unforgivingly
previous to me, grudging
the way I breathe their
property, the air,
speaking a twisted dialect to my differently-
shaped ears

though I tried to adapt

(the girl in a red tattered
petticoat, who jeered at me for my burned bread

Go back where you came from

I tightened my lips; knew that England
was now unreachable, had sunk down into the sea
without ever teaching me about washtubs)

got used to being
a minor invalid, expected to make
inept remarks,
futile and spastic gestures

(asked the Indian
about the squat thing on a stick
drying by the fire: Is that a toad?
Annoyed, he said No no,
deer liver, very good)

Finally I grew a chapped tarpaulin
skin; I negotiated the drizzle
of strange meaning, set it
down to just the latitude:
something to be endured
but not surprised by.

Inaccurate. The forest can still trick me:
one afternoon while I was drawing
birds, a malignant face
flickered over my shoulder;
the branches quivered.

Resolve: to be both tentative and hard to startle
(though clumsiness and
fright are inevitable)

in this area where my damaged
knowing of the language means
prediction is forever impossible

THE PLANTERS

They move between the jagged edge
of the forest and the jagged river
on a stumpy patch of cleared land

my husband, a neighbour, another man
weeding the few rows
of string beans and dusty potatoes.

They bend, straighten; the sun
lights up their faces and hands, candles
flickering in the wind against the

unbright earth. I see them; I know
none of them believe they are here.
They deny the ground they stand on,

pretend this dirt is the future.
And they are right. If they let go
of that illusion solid to them as a shovel,

open their eyes even for a moment
to these trees, to this particular sun
they would be surrounded, stormed, broken

in upon by branches, roots, tendrils, the dark
side of light
as I am.

THE WEREMAN

My husband walks in the frosted field
an X, a concept
defined against a blank;
he swerves, enters the forest
and is blotted out.

Unheld by my sight
what does he change into
what other shape
blends with the under-
growth, wavers across the pools
is camouflaged from the listening
swamp animals

At noon he will
return; or it may be
only my idea of him
I will find returning
with him hiding behind it.

He may change me also
with the fox eye, the owl
eye, the eightfold
eye of the spider

I can't think
what he will see
when he opens the door

PATHS AND THINGSCAPE

Those who went ahead
of us in the forest
bent the early trees
so that they grew to signals:

the trail was not
among the trees but
the trees

and there are some who have dreams
of birds flying in the shapes
of letters; the sky's
codes;
    and dream also
the significance of numbers (count
petals of certain flowers)

    In the morning I advance
    through the doorway: the sun
    on the bark, the inter-
    twisted branches, here
    a blue movement in the leaves, dispersed
    calls/ no trails; rocks
    and grey tufts of moss

The petals of the fire-
weed fall where they fall

I am watched like an invader
who knows hostility but
not where

The day shrinks back from me

When will be
that union and each
thing (bits
of surface broken by my foot
step) will without moving move
around me
into its place

THE TWO FIRES

One, the summer fire
outside: the trees melting, returning
to their first red elements
on all sides, cutting me off
from escape or the saving
lake

I sat in the house, raised up
between that shapeless raging
and my sleeping children
a charm: concentrate on
form, geometry, the human
architecture of the house, square
closed doors, proved roofbeams,
the logic of windows

(the children could not be wakened:
in their calm dreaming
the trees were straight and still
had branches and were green)

The other, the winter
fire inside: the protective roof
shrivelling overhead, the rafters
incandescent, all those corners
and straight lines flaming, the carefully-
made structure
prisoning us in a cage of blazing
bars
        the children
were awake and crying;

I wrapped them, carried them
outside into the snow.
Then I tried to rescue
what was left of their scorched dream
about the house: blankets,
warm clothes, the singed furniture
of safety cast away with them
in a white chaos

Two fires in-
formed me,

(each refuge fails
us; each danger
becomes a haven)

left charred marks
now around which I
try to grow

LOOKING IN A MIRROR

It was as if I woke
after a sleep of seven years

to find stiff lace, religious
black rotted
off by earth and the strong waters

and instead my skin thickened
with bark and the white hairs of roots

My heirloom face I brought
with me a crushed eggshell
among other debris:
the china plate shattered
on the forest road, the shawl
from India decayed, pieces of letters

and the sun here had stained
me its barbarous colour

Hands grown stiff, the fingers
brittle as twigs
eyes bewildered after
seven years, and almost
blind/ buds, which can see
only the wind

the mouth cracking
open like a rock in fire
trying to say

What is this

(you find only
the shape you already are
but what
if you have forgotten that
or discover you
have never known)

DEPARTURE FROM THE BUSH

I, who had been erased
by fire, was crept in
upon by green
                    (how
lucid a season)

            In time the animals
arrived to inhabit me,

first one
  by one, stealthily
(their habitual traces
burnt); then
having marked new boundaries
returning, more
confident, year
by year, two
by two

but restless: I was not ready
altogether to be moved into

They could tell I was
too heavy: I might
capsize;

I was frightened
by their eyes (green or
amber) glowing out from inside me

I was not completed; at night
I could not see without lanterns.

He wrote, We are leaving. I said
I have no clothes
left I can wear

The snow came. The sleigh was a relief;
its track lengthened behind,
pushing me towards the city

and rounding the first hill, I was
(instantaneous)
unlived in: they had gone.

There was something they almost taught me
I came away not having learned.

DEATH OF A YOUNG SON BY DROWNING

He, who navigated with success
the dangerous river of his own birth
once more set forth

on a voyage of discovery
into the land I floated on
but could not touch to claim.

His feet slid on the bank,
the currents took him;
he swirled with ice and trees in the swollen water

and plunged into distant regions,
his head a bathysphere;
through his eyes' thin glass bubbles

he looked out, reckless adventurer
on a landscape stranger than Uranus
we have all been to and some remember.

There was an accident; the air locked,
he was hung in the river like a heart.
They retrieved the swamped body,

cairn of my plans and future charts,
with poles and hooks
from among the nudging logs.

It was spring, the sun kept shining, the new grass
lept to solidity;
my hands glistened with details.

After the long trip I was tired of waves.
My foot hit rock. The dreamed sails
collapsed, ragged.

       I planted him in this country
       like a flag.

THE IMMIGRANTS

They are allowed to inherit
the sidewalks involved as palmlines, bricks
exhausted and soft, the deep
lawnsmells, orchards whorled
to the land's contours, the inflected weather

only to be told they are too poor
to keep it up, or someone
has noticed and wants to kill them; or the towns
pass laws which declare them obsolete.

I see them coming
up from the hold smelling of vomit,
infested, emaciated, their skins grey
with travel; as they step on shore

the old countries recede, become
perfect, thumbnail castles preserved
like gallstones in a glass bottle, the
towns dwindle upon the hillsides
in a light paperweight-clear.

They carry their carpetbags and trunks
with clothes, dishes, the family pictures;
they think they will make an order
like the old one, sow miniature orchards,
carve children and flocks out of wood

but always they are too poor, the sky
is flat, the green fruit shrivels
in the prairie sun, wood is for burning;
and if they go back, the towns

in time have crumbled, their tongues
stumble among awkward teeth, their ears
are filled with the sound of breaking glass.
I wish I could forget them
and so forget myself:

my mind is a wide pink map
across which move year after year
arrows and dotted lines, further and further,
people in railway cars

their heads stuck out of the windows
at stations, drinking milk or singing,
their features hidden with beards or shawls
day and night riding across an ocean of unknown
land to an unknown land.

DREAM 1 : THE BUSH GARDEN

I stood once more in that garden
sold, deserted and
gone to seed

In the dream I could
see down through the earth, could see
the potatoes curled
like pale grubs in the soil
the radishes thrusting down
their fleshy snouts, the beets
pulsing like slow amphibian hearts

Around my feet
the strawberries were surging, huge
and shining

When I bent
to pick, my hands
came away red and wet

In the dream I said
I should have known
anything planted here
would come up blood

One of the
things I found out by being
there, and after:

that history (that list
of ballooning wishes, flukes,
bent times, plunges and mistakes
clutched like parachutes)

is rolling itself up in your head
at one end and unrolling at the other

that this war will soon be among
those tiny ancestral figures
flickering dull white through the back of your skull,
confused, anxious, not sure any more
what they are doing there

appearing from time to time
with idiot faces and hands clusters
of bananas, holding flags,
holding guns, advancing through the trees
brown line green scribble

or crouching within a rough grey
crayon diagram of a fort,
shooting at each other, the smoke and red fire
made actual through a child's fingers.

DREAM 2 : BRIAN THE STILL-HUNTER

The man I saw in the forest
used to come to our house
every morning, never said anything;
I learned from the neighbours later
he once tried to cut his throat.

I found him at the end of the path
sitting on a fallen tree
cleaning his gun.

There was no wind;
around us the leaves rustled.

He said to me:
I kill because I have to

but every time I aim, I feel
my skin grow fur
my head heavy with antlers
and during the stretched instant
the bullet glides on its thread of speed
my soul runs innocent as hooves.

Is God just to his creatures?

I die more often than many.

He looked up and I saw
the white scar made by the hunting knife
around his neck.

When I woke
I remembered: he has been gone
twenty years and not heard from.

CHARIVARI

'They capped their heads with feathers, masked
their faces, wore their clothes backwards, howled
with torches through the midnight winter

and dragged the black man from his house
to the jolting music of broken
instruments, pretending to each other

it was a joke, until
they killed him. I don't know
what happened to the white bride.'

The American lady, adding she
thought it was a disgraceful piece
of business, finished her tea.

(Note: Never pretend this isn't
part of the soil too, teadrinkers, and inadvertent
victims and murderers, when we come this way

again in other forms, take care
to look behind, within
where the skeleton face beneath

the face puts on its feather mask, the arm
within the arm lifts up the spear:
Resist those cracked

drumbeats. Stop this. Become human.)

DREAM 3: NIGHT BEAR
WHICH FRIGHTENED CATTLE

Horns crowding toward us
a stampede of bellowing, one
night the surface of my mind keeps
only as anecdote

We laughed, safe with lanterns
at the kitchen door

though beneath stories

where forgotten birds
tremble through memory, ripples across water
and a moon hovers in the lake
orange and prehistoric

I lean with my feet grown intangible
because I am not there

watching the bear I didn't see condense
itself among the trees, an outline
tenuous as an echo

but it is real, heavier
than real   I know
even by daylight here
in this visible kitchen

it absorbs all terror

it moves toward the lighted cabin
below us on the slope
where my family gathers

a mute vibration passing
between my ears

THE DEATHS OF THE OTHER CHILDREN

The body dies

little by little

the body buries itself

joins itself
to the loosened mind, to the black-
berries and thistles, running in a
thorny wind
over the shallow
foundations of our former houses,
dim hollows now in the sandy soil

Did I spend all those years
building up this edifice
my composite
                 self, this crumbling hovel?

My arms, my eyes, my grieving
words, my disintegrated children

Everywhere I walk, along
the overgrowing paths, my skirt
tugged at by the spreading briers

they catch at my heels with their fingers

THE DOUBLE VOICE

Two voices
took turns using my eyes:

One had manners,
painted in watercolours,
used hushed tones when speaking
of mountains or Niagara Falls,
composed uplifting verse
and expended sentiment upon the poor.

The other voice
had other knowledge:
that men sweat
always and drink often,
that pigs are pigs
but must be eaten
anyway, that unborn babies
fester like wounds in the body,
that there is nothing to be done
about mosquitoes;

One saw through my
bleared and gradually
bleaching eyes, red leaves,
the rituals of seasons and rivers

The other found a dead dog
jubilant with maggots
half-buried among the sweet peas.

LATER IN BELLEVILLE: CAREER

Once by a bitter candle
of oil and braided
rags, I wrote
verses about love and sleighbells

which I exchanged for potatoes;

in the summers I painted butterflies
on a species of white fungus
which were bought by the tourists, glass-
cased for English parlours

and my children (miraculous)
wore shoes.

Now every day
I sit on a stuffed sofa
in my own fringed parlour, have
uncracked plates (from which I eat
at intervals)
and a china teaset.

There is no use for art.

DAGUERREOTYPE TAKEN IN OLD AGE

I know I change
have changed

but whose is this vapid face
pitted and vast, rotund
suspended in empty paper
as though in a telescope

the granular moon

I rise from my chair
pulling against gravity
I turn away
and go out into the garden

I revolve among the vegetables,
my head ponderous
reflecting the sun
in shadows from the pocked ravines
cut in my cheeks, my eye-
sockets 2 craters

along the paths
I orbit
the apple trees
white white spinning
stars around me

I am being
eaten away by light

WISH: METAMORPHOSIS
TO HERALDIC EMBLEM

I balance myself carefully
inside my shrinking body
which is nevertheless
deceptive as a cat's fur:

when I am dipped in the earth
I will be much smaller.

On my skin the wrinkles branch
out, overlapping like hair or feathers.

In this parlour my grandchildren
uneasy on sunday chairs
with my deafness, my cameo brooch
my puckered mind
scurrying in its old burrows

little guess how
                    maybe

I will prowl and slink
in crystal darkness
among the stalactite roots, with new
formed plumage
                    uncorroded
                              gold and

Fiery green, my fingers
curving and scaled, my

opal
     no
  eyes glowing

VISIT TO TORONTO, WITH COMPANIONS

The streets are new, the harbour
is new also;
the lunatic asylum is yellow.

On the first floor there were
women sitting, sewing;
they looked at us sadly, gently,
answered questions.

On the second floor there were
women crouching, thrashing,
tearing off their clothes, screaming;
to us they paid little attention.

On the third floor
I went through a glass-panelled
door into a different kind of room.
It was a hill, with boulders, trees, no houses.
I sat down and smoothed my gloves.

The landscape was saying something
but I couldn't hear. One of the rocks
sighed and rolled over.

Above me, at eye level
three faces appeared in an oblong space.

They wanted me to go out
to where there were streets and
the Toronto harbour

I shook my head. There were no clouds, the flowers
deep red and feathered, shot from among
the dry stones,
                    the air
was about to tell me
all kinds of answers

SOLIPSISM WHILE DYING

the skeleton produces flesh   enemy
                                                    opposing, then taken
                                                    for granted, earth harvested, used
                                                    up, walked over

the ears produce sounds   what I heard I
                                                created. (voices
                                                determining, repeating
                                                histories, worn customs

the mouth produces words   I said I created
                                                    myself, and these
                                                    frames, commas, calendars
                                                    that enclose me

the hands produce objects   the world touched
                                                    into existence: was
                                                    this cup, this village here
                                                    before my fingers

the eyes produce light   the sky
                                leaps at me: let there be
                                the sun-
                                set

Or so I thought, lying in the bed
being regretted

added: What will they do now
that I, that all
depending on me disappears?

Where will be Belleville?

        Kingston?

        (the fields
         I held between. the lake
         boats

            toro N T O

THOUGHTS FROM UNDERGROUND

When I first reached this country
I hated it
and I hated it more each year:

in summer the light a
violent blur, the heat
thick as a swamp,
the green things fiercely
shoving themselves upwards, the
eyelids bitten by insects

In winter our teeth were brittle
with cold. We fed on squirrels.
At night the house cracked.
In the mornings, we thawed
the bad bread over the stove.

Then we were made successful
and I felt I ought to love
this country.
                    I said I loved it
and my mind saw double.

I began to forget myself
in the middle
of sentences. Events
were split apart

I fought. I constructed
desperate paragraphs of praise, everyone
ought to love it because

and set them up at intervals

      due to natural resources, native industry, superior
      penitentiaries
      we will all be rich and powerful

flat as highway billboards

      who can doubt it, look how
      fast Belleville is growing

(though it is still no place for an english gentleman)

ALTERNATE THOUGHTS
FROM UNDERGROUND

      Down. Shovelled. Can hear
      faintly laughter, footsteps;
      the shrill of glass and steel

      the invaders of those for whom
      shelter was wood,
      fire was terror and sacred

      the inheritors, the raisers
      of glib superstructures.

My heart silted by decades
of older thoughts, yet prays

O topple this glass pride, fireless
rivetted babylon, prays
through subsoil
to my wooden fossil God.

But they prevail. Extinct. I feel
scorn but also pity: what
the bones of the giant reptiles

done under by the thing
(may call it
climate) outside the circle
they drew by their closed senses
of what was right

felt when scuttled
across, nested in by the velvet immoral
uncalloused and armourless mammals.

RESURRECTION

I see now I see
now I cannot see

earth is a blizzard in my eyes

I hear now

       the rustle of the snow

the angels listening above me

       thistles bright with sleet
       gathering

waiting for the time
to reach me
up to the pillared
sun, the final city

       or living towers

unrisen yet
whose dormant stones lie folding
their holy fire around me

       (but the land shifts with frost
       and those who have become the stone
       voices of the land
       shift also and say

god is not
the voice in the whirlwind

god is the whirlwind

at the last
judgement we will all be trees

A BUS ALONG ST CLAIR: DECEMBER

It would take more than that to banish
me: this is my kingdom still.

Turn, look up
through the gritty window: an unexplored
wilderness of wires

Though they buried me in monuments
of concrete slabs, of cables
though they mounded a pyramid
of cold light over my head
though they said, We will build
silver paradise with a bulldozer

it shows how little they know
about vanishing: I have
my ways of getting through.

Right now, the snow
is no more familiar
to you than it was to me:
this is my doing.
The grey air, the roar
going on behind it
are no more familiar.

I am the old woman
sitting across from you on the bus,
her shoulders drawn up like a shawl;
out of her eyes come secret
hatpins, destroying
the walls, the ceiling

Turn, look down:
there is no city;
this is the centre of a forest

your place is empty

From

Procedures for Underground

1970

GAME AFTER SUPPER

This is before electricity,
it is when there were porches.

On the sagging porch an old man
is rocking. The porch is wooden,

the house is wooden and grey;
in the living room which smells of
smoke and mildew, soon
the woman will light the kerosene lamp.

There is a barn but I am not in the barn;
there is an orchard too, gone bad,
its apples like soft cork
but I am not there either.

I am hiding in the long grass
with my two dead cousins,
the membrane grown already
across their throats.

We hear crickets and our own hearts
close to our ears;
though we giggle, we are afraid.

From the shadows around
the corner of the house
a tall man is coming to find us:

He will be an uncle,
if we are lucky.

GIRL AND HORSE, 1928

You are younger than I am, you are
someone I never knew, you stand
under a tree, your face half-shadowed,
holding the horse by its bridle.

Why do you smile?   Can't you
see the apple blossoms falling around
you, snow, sun, snow, listen, the tree
dries and is being burnt, the wind

is bending your body, your face
ripples like water   where did you go
But no, you stand there exactly
the same, you can't hear me, forty

years ago you were caught by light
and fixed in that secret
place where we live, where we believe
nothing can change, grow older.

                    (On the other side
                    of the picture, the instant
                    is over, the shadow
                    of the tree has moved. You wave,

                    then turn and ride
                    out of sight through the vanished
                    orchard, still smiling
                    as though you do not notice)

THE SMALL CABIN

The house we built gradually
from the ground up when we were young
(three rooms, the walls
raw trees) burned down
last year   they said

I didn't see it, and so
the house is still there in me

among branches as always   I stand
inside it looking out
at the rain moving across the lake

but when I go back
to the empty place in the forest
the house will blaze and crumple
suddenly in my mind

collapsing like a cardboard carton
thrown on a bonfire, summers
crackling, my earlier
selves outlined in flame.

Left in my head will be
the blackened earth: the truth.

Where did the house go?

Where do the words go
when we have said them?

MIDWINTER, PRESOLSTICE

The cold rises around
our house, the wind
drives through the walls in
splinters; on the inside
of the window, behind
the blanket we have hung
a white mould thickens.

We spend the days quietly
trying to be warm; we can't
look through the glass;
in the refrigerator old food
sickens, gives out.

I dream of departures, meetings,
repeated weddings with a stranger, wounded
with knives and bandaged, his
face hidden

                All night my gentle husband
sits alone in the corner
of a grey arena, guarding
a paper bag
                which holds
turnips and apples and my
head, the eyes closed

PROCEDURES FOR UNDERGROUND
(Northwest Coast)

The country beneath
the earth has a green sun
and the rivers flow backwards;

the trees and rocks are the same
as they are here, but shifted.
Those who live there are always hungry;

from them you can learn
wisdom and great power,
if you can descend and return safely.

You must look for tunnels, animal
burrows or the cave in the sea
guarded by the stone man;

when you are down you will find
those who were once your friends
but they will be changed and dangerous.

Resist them, be careful
never to eat their food.
Afterwards, if you live, you will be able

to see them when they prowl as winds,
as thin sounds in our village. You will
tell us their names, what they want, who

has made them angry by forgetting them.
For this gift, as for all gifts, you must
suffer: those from the underland

will be always with you, whispering their
complaints, beckoning you
back down; while among us here

you will walk wrapped in an invisible
cloak. Few will seek your help
with love, none without fear.

DREAMS OF THE ANIMALS

Mostly the animals dream
of other animals   each
according to its kind

      (though certain mice and small rodents
        have nightmares of a huge pink
        shape with five claws descending)

: moles dream of darkness and delicate
mole smells

frogs dream of green and golden
frogs
sparkling like wet suns
among the lilies

red and black
striped fish, their eyes open
have red and black striped
dreams   defence, attack, meaningful
patterns

birds dream of territories
enclosed by singing.

Sometimes the animals dream of evil
in the form of soap and metal
but mostly the animals dream
of other animals.

There are exceptions:

      the silver fox in the roadside zoo
      dreams of digging out
      and of baby foxes, their necks bitten

      the caged armadillo
      near the train
      station, which runs
      all day in figure eights
      its piglet feet pattering,
      no longer dreams
      but is insane when waking;

      the iguana
      in the petshop window on St Catherine Street
      crested, royal-eyed, ruling
      its kingdom of water-dish and sawdust

      dreams of sawdust.

CYCLOPS

You, going along the path,
mosquito-doped, with no moon, the flashlight
a single orange eye

unable to see what is beyond
the capsule of your dim
sight, what shape

contracts to a heart
with terror, bumps
among the leaves, what makes
a bristling noise like a fur throat

Is it true you do not wish to hurt them?

Is it true you have no fear?
Take off your shoes then,
let your eyes go bare,
swim in their darkness as in a river

do not disguise
yourself in armour.

They watch you from hiding:
you are a chemical
smell, a cold fire, you are
giant and indefinable

In their monstrous night
thick with possible claws
where danger is not knowing,

you are the hugest monster.

THREE DESK OBJECTS

What suns had to rise and set
what eyes had to blink out
what hands and fingers
had to let go of their heat

before you appeared on my desk
black light
portable and radiant

and you, my electric typewriter
with your cord and hungry plug
drinking a sinister transfusion
from the other side of the wall

what histories of slaughter
have left these scars on your keys

What multiple deaths have set loose this clock
the small wheels that grind
their teeth under the metal scalp

My cool machines
resting there so familiar
so hard and perfect

I am afraid to touch you
I think you will cry out in pain

I think you will be warm, like skin.

PROJECTED SLIDE
OF AN UNKNOWN SOLDIER

Upon the wall a face
uttered itself
in light, pushing
aside the wall's darkness;

Around it leaves, glossy,
perhaps tropical, not making
explicit whether the face was
breaking through them, wore them
as disguise, was crowned
with them or sent them
forth as rays,
a slippery halo;

The clothes were invisible,
the eyes
hidden; the nose
foreshortened: a muzzle.
Hair on the upper lip.
On the skin the light shone, wet
with heat; the teeth
of the open mouth reflected it
as absolute.

The mouth was open
stretched wide in a call or howl
(there was no tongue)
of agony, ultimate
command or simple famine.
The canine teeth ranged back
into the throat and vanished.

The mouth was filled with darkness.
The darkness in the open mouth
uttered itself, pushing
aside the light.

COMIC BOOKS VS. HISTORY
(1949, 1969)

On the blackboard map your country
was erased, blank, waiting
to be filled with whatever shapes
we chose:

       tense
needle turrets of steel
cities

       heroes
lived there, we knew

they all wore capes, bullets
bounced off them;
from their fists came beautiful
orange collisions.

Our side was coloured in
with dots and letters

but it held only
real-sized explorers, confined
to animal skin coats;

they plodded, discovered
rivers whose names we always
forgot; in the winters
they died of scurvy.

When I reached that other
shore finally, statistics
and diseased labels multiplied
everywhere in my head

space contracted, the
red and silver
heroes had collapsed inside
their rubber suits / the riddled
buildings were decaying
magic

I turn back, search
for the actual, collect lost
bones, burnt logs
of campfires, pieces of fur.

HIGHEST ALTITUDE

Here, our possessions are cut
to what we carry: plates,

blanket, our maps, basket with food,
last thought: lake where we waded
in the green glacial water.

The view to the side, below,
would be, as they say, breath-

taking; if we dared to look.
We don't dare. The curved

ledge is crumbling, the melting snow
is undermining the road,

in fear everything
lives, impermanence
makes the edges of things burn

brighter. The rocks are purple, heart-
red. We hold our eyes tight
to the line; the reference point

not the mountains but the moving
car, and each other.

A MORNING

Because we couldn't sleep we went on
though at first I could see little;

behind us the sun rose
white and cold; the early
wind came out of the sun.

In front of us the low hills, yellow-
grey grass dunes, and then
the mountains: hard, furrowed
with erosion, cloudless, old, new,
abrupt in the first light.

With shrunken fingers
we ate our oranges and bread,
shivering in the parked car;

though we knew we had never
been there before,
we knew we had been there before.

A SOUL, GEOLOGICALLY

The longer we stay here the harder
it is for me to see you.

Your outline, skin
that marks you off
melts in this light

and from behind your face
the unknown areas appear:

hills yellow-pelted, dried earth
bubbles, or thrust up
steeply as knees

the sky a flat blue desert,

these spaces you fill
with their own emptiness.

Your shape wavers, glares
like heat above the road,

then you merge and extend:
you have gone,
in front of me there is a stone ridge.

Which of these forms
have you taken:

hill, tree clawed
to the rock, fallen rocks worn
and rounded by the wind

You are the wind,
you contain me

I walk in the white silences
of your mind, remembering

the way it is millions of years before
on the wide floor of the sea

while my eyes lift like continents
to the sun and erode slowly.

HABITATION

Marriage is not
a house or even a tent

it is before that, and colder:

the edge of the forest, the edge
of the desert
                the unpainted stairs
at the back where we squat
outside, eating popcorn

the edge of the receding glacier

where painfully and with wonder
at having survived even
this far

we are learning to make fire

WOMAN SKATING

A lake sunken among
cedar and black spruce hills;
late afternoon.

On the ice a woman skating,
jacket sudden
red against the white,

concentrating on moving
in perfect circles.

> (actually she is my mother, she is
> over at the outdoor skating rink
> near the cemetery. On three sides
> of her there are streets of brown
> brick houses; cars go by; on the
> fourth side is the park building.
> The snow banked around the rink
> is grey with soot. She never skates
> here. She's wearing a sweater and
> faded maroon earmuffs, she has
> taken off her gloves)

Now near the horizon
the enlarged pink sun swings down.
Soon it will be zero.

With arms wide the skater
turns, leaving her breath like a diver's
trail of bubbles.

Seeing the ice
as what it is, water:

seeing the months
as they are, the years
in sequence occurring
underfoot, watching
the miniature human
figure balanced on steel
needles (those compasses
floated in saucers) on time
sustained, above
time circling: miracle

Over all I place
a glass bell

YOUNGER SISTER, GOING SWIMMING
(Northern Quebec)

Beside this lake
where there are no other people

my sister in bathing suit continues
her short desolate
parade to the end of the dock;

against the boards
her feet make sad statements
she thinks no one can hear;

(I sit in a deckchair
not counting, invisible;
the sun wavers on
this page as on a pool.)

She moves the raft out
past the sandy point;
no one comes by in a motorboat.

She would like to fill the lake
with other swimmers, with answers.
She calls her name. The sun encloses
rocks, trees, her feet in the water, the circling
bays and hills as before.

She poises, raises her arms
as though signalling, then disappears.
The lake heals itself quietly
of the wound left by the diver.
The air quakes and is still.

(Under my hand the paper
closes over these
marks I am making on it.

The words ripple, subside,
move outwards toward the shore.)

FISHING FOR EEL TOTEMS

I stood on the reed bank
ear tuned to the line, listening
to the signals from the ones who lived
under the blue barrier,

thinking they had no words for things
in the air.

The string jumped,
I hooked a martian / it poured
fluid silver out of the river

its long body whipped on the grass, reciting
all the letters of its alphabet.

Killed, it was a
grey tongue hanged silent in the smokehouse

which we later ate.

After that I could see
for a time in the green country;

I learned that the earliest language
was not our syntax of chained pebbles

but liquid, made
by the first tribes, the fish
people.

BUFFALO IN COMPOUND: ALBERTA

The marsh flat where they graze
beside the stream is
late afternoon, serene
with slanted light: green leaves are
yellow: even
the mud shines

Placid, they bend down
silently to the grass;
when they move, the small birds
follow, settle almost
under their feet.

Fenced out but anxious
anyway, and glad our car is
near, we press
close to the wire
squares, our hands raised
for shields
against the sun, which is
everywhere

       It was hard to see them
but we thought we saw
in the field near them, the god
of this place: brutal,
zeus-faced, his horned
head man-bearded, his
fused red eye turned inward
to cloudburst and pounded earth, the water-
falling of hooves fisted inside
a calm we would call madness.

Then they were going
in profile, one by one, their
firelit outlines fixed as carvings

backs to us now
they enter
the shade of the gold-edged trees

CARRYING FOOD HOME IN WINTER

I walk uphill through the snow
hard going
brown paper bag of groceries
balanced low on my stomach,
heavy, my arms stretching
to hold it turn all tendon.

Do we need this paper bag
my love, do we need this bulk
of peels and cores, do we need
these bottles, these roots
and bits of cardboard
to keep us floating
as on a raft
above the snow I sink through?

The skin creates
islands of warmth
in winter, in summer
islands of coolness.

The mouth performs
a similar deception.

I say I will transform
this egg into a muscle
this bottle into an act of love

This onion will become a motion
this grapefruit
will become a thought.

From

Power Politics

1971

you fit into me
like a hook into an eye

a fish hook
an open eye

You take my hand and
I'm suddenly in a bad movie,
it goes on and on and
why am I fascinated

We waltz in slow motion
through an air stale with aphorisms
we meet behind endless potted palms
you climb through the wrong windows

Other people are leaving
but I always stay till the end
I paid my money, I
want to see what happens.

In chance bathtubs I have to
peel you off me
in the form of smoke and melted
celluloid

Have to face it I'm
finally an addict,
the smell of popcorn and worn plush
lingers for weeks

I can change my-
self more easily
than I can change you

I could grow bark and
become a shrub

or switch back in time
to the woman image left
in cave rubble, the drowned
stomach bulbed with fertility,
face a tiny bead, a
lump, queen of the termites

or (better) speed myself up,
disguise myself in the knuckles
and purple-veined veils of old ladies,
become arthritic and genteel

or one twist further:
collapse across your
bed clutching my heart
and pull the nostalgic sheet up over
my waxed farewell smile

which would be inconvenient
but final.

In restaurants we argue
over which of us will pay for your funeral

though the real question is
whether or not I will make you immortal.

At the moment only I
can do it and so

I raise the magic fork
over the plate of beef fried rice

and plunge it into your heart.
There is a faint pop, a sizzle

and through your own split head
you rise up glowing;

the ceiling opens
a voice sings Love Is A Many

Splendoured Thing
you hang suspended above the city

in blue tights and a red cape,
your eyes flashing in unison.

The other diners regard you
some with awe, some only with bordom:

they cannot decide if you are a new weapon
or only a new advertisement.

As for me, I continue eating;
I liked you better the way you were,
but you were always ambitious.

After the agony in the guest
bedroom, you lying by the
overturned bed
your face uplifted, neck propped
against the windowsill, my arm
under you, cold moon
shining down through the window

wine mist rising
around you, an almost-
visible halo

You say, Do you
love me, do you love me

I answer you:
I stretch your arms out
one to either side,
your head slumps forward.

Later I take you home
in a taxi, and you
are sick in the bathtub

My beautiful wooden leader
with your heartful of medals
made of wood, fixing it
each time so you almost win,

you long to be bandaged
before you have been cut.
My love for you is the love
of one statue for another: tensed

and static. General, you enlist
my body in your heroic
struggle to become real:
though you promise bronze rescues

you hold me by the left ankle
so that my head brushes the ground,
my eyes are blinded,
my hair fills with white ribbons.

There are hordes of me now, alike
and paralyzed, we follow you
scattering floral tributes
under your hooves.

Magnificent on your wooden horse
you point with your fringed hand;
the sun sets, and the people all
ride off in the other direction.

You want to go back
to where the sky was inside us

animals ran through us, our hands
blessed and killed according to our
wisdom, death
made real blood come out

But face it, we have been
improved, our heads float
several inches above our necks
moored to us by
rubber tubes and filled with
clever bubbles,

                      our bodies
are populated with billions
of soft pink numbers
multiplying and analyzing
themselves, perfecting
their own demands, no trouble to anyone.

I love you by
sections and when you work.

Do you want to be illiterate?
This is the way it is, get used to it.

i

To understand
each other: anything
but that, & to avoid it

I will suspend my search for
germs if you will keep
your fingers off the microfilm
hidden inside my skin

ii

I approach this love
like a biologist
pulling on my rubber
gloves & white labcoat

You flee from it
like an escaped political
prisoner, and no wonder

iii

You held out your hand
I took your fingerprints

You asked for love
I gave you only descriptions

Please die I said
so I can write about it

After all you are quite
ordinary: 2 arms 2 legs
a head, a reasonable
body, toes & fingers, a few
eccentricities, a few honesties
but not too many, too many
postponements & regrets but

you'll adjust to it, meeting
deadlines and other
people, pretending to love
the wrong woman some of the
time, listening to your brain
shrink, your diaries
expanding as you grow older,

growing older, of course you'll
die but not yet, you'll outlive
even my distortions of you

and there isn't anything
I want to do about the fact
that you are unhappy & sick

you aren't sick & unhappy
only alive & stuck with it.

yes at first you
go down smooth as
pills, all of me
breathes you in and then it's

a kick in the head, orange
and brutal, sharp jewels
hit and my
hair splinters

        the adjectives
fall away from me, no
threads left holding
me, I flake apart
layer by
layer down
quietly to the bone, my skull
unfolds to an astounded flower

regrowing the body, learning
speech again takes
days and longer
each time / too much of
this is fatal

i

We are hard on each other
and call it honesty,
choosing our jagged truths
with care and aiming them across
the neutral table.

The things we say are
true; it is our crooked
aims, our choices
turn them criminal.

ii

Of course your lies
are more amusing:
you make them new each time.

Your truths, painful and boring
repeat themselves over & over
perhaps because you own
so few of them

iii

A truth should exist,
it should not be used
like this. If I love you

is that a fact or a weapon?

iv

Does the body lie
moving like this, are these
touches, hairs, wet
soft marble my tongue runs over
lies you are telling me?

Your body is not a word,
it does not lie or
speak truth either.

It is only
here or not here.

At first I was given centuries
to wait in caves, in leather
tents, knowing you would never come back

Then it speeded up: only
several years between
the day you jangled off
into the mountains, and the day (it was
spring again) I rose from the embroidery
frame at the messenger's entrance.

That happened twice, or was it
more; and there was once, not so
long ago, you failed,
and came back in a wheelchair
with a moustache and a sunburn
and were insufferable.

Time before last though, I remember
I had a good eight months between
running alongside the train, skirts hitched, handing
you violets in at the window
and opening the letter; I watched
your snapshot fade for twenty years.

And last time (I drove to the airport
still dressed in my factory
overalls, the wrench
I had forgotten sticking out of the back
pocket; there you were,
zippered and helmeted, it was zero
hour, you said Be
Brave) it was at least three weeks before
I got the telegram and could start regretting.

But recently, the bad evenings
there are only seconds
between the warning on the radio and the
explosion; my hands
don't reach you

and on quieter nights
you jump up from
your chair without even touching your dinner
and I can scarcely kiss you goodbye
before you run out into the street and they shoot

You refuse to own
yourself, you permit
others to do it for you:

you become slowly more public,
in a year there will be nothing left
of you but a megaphone

or you will descend through the roof
with the spurious authority of a
government official,
blue as a policeman, grey as a used angel,
having long forgotten the difference
between an annunciation and a parking ticket

or you will be slipped under
the door, your skin furred with cancelled
airmail stamps, your kiss no longer literature
but fine print, a set of instructions.

If you deny these uniforms
and choose to repossess
yourself, your future

will be less dignified, more painful, death will be sooner,
(it is no longer possible
to be both human and alive) : lying piled with
the others, your face and body
covered so thickly with scars
only the eyes show through.

We hear nothing these days
from the ones in power

Why talk when you are a shoulder
or a vault

Why talk when you are
helmeted with numbers

Fists have many forms;
a fist knows what it can do

without the nuisance of speaking:
it grabs and smashes.

From those inside or under
words gush like toothpaste.

Language, the fist
proclaims by squeezing
is for the weak only.

You did it
it was you who started the countdown

and you conversely
on whom the demonic number
zero descended in the form of an egg-
bodied machine
coming at you like a
football or a bloated thumb

and it was you whose skin
fell off bubbling
all at once when the fence
accidentally touched you

and you also who laughed
when you saw it happen,

When will you learn
the flame and the wood/flesh
it burns are whole and the same?

You attempt merely power
you accomplish merely suffering

How long do you expect me to wait
while you cauterize your
senses, one
after another
turning yourself to an
impervious glass tower?

How long will you demand I love you?

I'm through, I won't make
any more flowers for you

I judge you as the trees do
by dying

This is a mistake,
these arms and legs
that don't work any more

Now it's broken
and no space for excuses.

The earth doesn't comfort,
it only covers up
if you have the decency to stay quiet

The sun doesn't forgive,
it looks and keeps going.

Night seeps into us
through the accidents we have
inflicted on each other

Next time we commit
love, we ought to
choose in advance what to kill.

Beyond truth,
tenacity: of those
dwarf trees & mosses,
hooked into straight rock
believing the sun's lies & thus
refuting / gravity

& of this cactus, gathering
itself together
against the sand, yes tough
rind & spikes but doing
the best it can

⚓ *They are hostile nations*

i

In view of the fading animals
the proliferation of sewers and fears
the sea clogging, the air
nearing extinction

we should be kind, we should
take warning, we should forgive each other

Instead we are opposite, we
touch as though attacking,

the gifts we bring
even in good faith maybe
warp in our hands to
implements, to manoeuvres

ii

Put down the target of me
you guard inside your binoculars,
in turn I will surrender

this aerial photograph
(your vulnerable
sections marked in red)
I have found so useful

See, we are alone in
the dormant field, the snow
that cannot be eaten or captured

iii

Here there are no armies
here there is no money

It is cold and getting colder

We need each others'
breathing, warmth, surviving
is the only war
we can afford, stay

walking with me, there is almost
time / if we can only
make it as far as

the (possibly) last summer

Spring again, can I stand it
shooting its needles into
the earth, my head, both
used to darkness

Snow on brown soil and
the squashed caterpillar
coloured liquid lawn

Winter collapses
in slack folds around
my feet / no leaves yet / loose fat

Thick lilac buds crouch for the
spurt but I
hold back

Not ready / help me
what I want from you is
moonlight smooth as
wind, long hairs of water

I am sitting on the
edge of the impartial
bed, I have been turned to crystal, you enter

bringing love in the form of
a cardboard box (empty)
a pocket (empty)
some hands (also empty)

Be careful I say but
how can you
                the empty
thing comes out of your hands, it
fills the room slowly, it is
a pressure, a lack of
pressure
            Like a deep sea
creature with glass bones and wafer
eyes drawn
to the surface, I break

open, the pieces of me
shine briefly in your empty hands

I see you fugitive, stumbling across the prairie,
lungs knotted by thirst, sunheat
nailing you down, all the things
after you that can be after you
with their clamps and poisoned mazes

Should I help you?
Should I make you a mirage?

My right hand unfolds rivers
around you, my left hand releases its trees,
I speak rain,
I spin you a night and you hide in it.

Now you have one enemy
instead of many.

What is it, it does not
move like love, it does
not want to know, it
does not want to stroke, unfold

it does not even want to
touch, it is more like
an animal (not
loving) a
thing trapped, you move
wounded, you are hurt, you hurt,
you want to get out, you want
to tear yourself out, I am

the outside, I am snow and
space, pathways, you gather
yourself, your muscles

clutch, you move
into me as though I
am (wrenching
your way through, this is
urgent, it is your
life) the
last chance for freedom

You are the sun
in reverse, all energy
flows into you and is
abolished; you refuse
houses, you smell of
catastrophe, I see you
blind and one-handed, flashing
in the dark, trees breaking
under your feet, you demand,
you demand

I lie mutilated beside
you; beneath us there are
sirens, fires, the people run
squealing, the city
is crushed and gutted,
the ends of your fingers bleed
from 1000 murders

Putting on my clothes
again, retreating, closing doors
I am amazed / I can continue
to think, eat, anything

How can I stop you

Why did I create you

i

I'm telling the wrong lies,
they are not even useful.

The right lies would at least
be keys, they would open the door.

The door is closed; the chairs,
the tables, the steel bowl, myself

shaping bread in the kitchen, wait
outside it.

ii

That was a lie also,
I could go in if I wanted to.

Whose house is this
we both live in
but neither of us owns

How can I be expected
to find my way around

I could go in if I wanted to,
that's not the point, I don't have time,

I should be doing something
other than you.

iii

What do you want from me
you who walk towards me over the long floor

your arms outstretched, your heart
luminous through the ribs

around your head a crown
of shining blood

This is your castle, this is your metal door,
these are your stairs, your

bones, you twist all possible
dimensions into your own

iv

Alternate version: you advance
through the grey streets of this house,

the walls crumble, the dishes
thaw, vines grow
on the softening refrigerator

I say, leave me
alone, this is my winter,

I will stay here if I choose

You will not listen
to resistances, you cover me

with flags, a dark red
season, you delete from me
all other colours

v

Don't let me do this to you,
you are not those other people,
you are yourself

Take off the signatures, the false
bodies, this love
which does not fit you

This is not a house, there are no doors,
get out while it is
open, while you still can

vi

If we make stories for each other
about what is in the room
we will never have to go in.

You say: my other wives
are in there, they are all
beautiful and happy, they love me, why
disturb them

I say: it is only
a cupboard, my collection
of envelopes, my painted
eggs, my rings

In your pockets the thin women
hang on their hooks, dismembered

Around my neck I wear
the head of the beloved, pressed
in the metal retina like a picked flower.

vii

Should we go into it
together / If I go into it
with you I will never come out

If I wait outside I can salvage
this house or what is left
of it, I can keep
my candles, my dead uncles
my restrictions

but you will go
alone, either
way is loss

Tell me what it is for

In the room we will find nothing
In the room we will find each other

Lying here, everything in me
brittle and pushing you away

This is not something I
wanted, I tell you

silently, not admitting
the truth of where

I am, so far
up, the sky incredible and dark

blue, each breath
a gift in the steep air

How hard even the boulders
find it to grow here

and I don't know how to accept
your freedom, I don't know

what to do with this
precipice, this joy

What do you see, I ask / my voice
absorbed by stone and outer

space / you are asleep, you see
what there is. Beside you

I bend and enter

I look up, you are standing
on the other side of the window

now   your body
glimmers in the dark

room / you rise above me
smooth, chill, stone-

white / you smell of tunnels
you smell of too much time

I should have used leaves
and silver to prevent you

instead I summoned

you are not a bird you do not fly
you are not an animal you do not run

you are not a man

your mouth is nothingness
where it touches me I vanish

you descend on me like age
you descend on me like earth

I can't tell you my name:
you don't believe I have one

I can't warn you this boat is falling
you planned it that way

You've never had a face
but you know that appeals to me

You are old enough to be my
skeleton: you know that also.

I can't tell you I don't want you
the sea is on your side

You have the earth's nets
I have only a pair of scissors.

When I look for you I find
water or moving shadow

There is no way I can lose you
when you are lost already.

They were all inaccurate:

the hinged bronze man, the fragile man
built of glass pebbles,
the fanged man with his opulent capes and boots

peeling away from you in scales.

It was my fault but you helped,
you enjoyed it.

Neither of us will enjoy
the rest: you following me
down streets, hallways, melting
when I touch you,
avoiding the sleeves of the bargains
I hold out for you,
your face corroded by truth,

crippled, persistent.You ask
like the wind, again and again and
wordlessly, for the one forbidden thing:

love without mirrors and not for
my reasons but your own.

From
You Are Happy
1974

NEWSREEL: MAN AND FIRING SQUAD

i

A botched job,
the blindfold slipped, he sees
his own death approaching, says No
or something, his torso jumps as the bullets hit
his nerves / he slopes down,
wrecked and not even
cleanly, roped muscles leaping, mouth open
as though snoring, the photography
isn't good either.

ii

Destruction shines with such beauty

Light on his wet hair
serpents of blood jerked from the wrists

Sun thrown from the raised and lowered
rifles / debris of the still alive

Your left eye, green and lethal

iii

We depart, we say goodbye

Yet each of us remains in the same place,
staked out and waiting,
it is the ground between that moves, expands,
pulling us away from each other.

No more of these closeups, this agony
taken just for the record anyway

The scenery is rising behind us
into focus, the walls
and hills are also important,

Our shattered faces retreat, we might be
happy, who can interpret
the semaphore of our bending
bodies, from a distance we could be dancing

NOVEMBER

i

This creature kneeling
dusted with snow, its teeth
grinding together, sound of old stones
at the bottom of a river

You lugged it to the barn
I held the lantern,
we leaned over it
as if it were being born.

ii

The sheep hangs upside down from the rope,
a long fruit covered with wool and rotting.
It waits for the dead wagon
to harvest it.

Mournful November
this is the image
you invent for me,
the dead sheep came out of your head, a legacy:

Kill what you can't save
what you can't eat throw out
what you can't throw out bury

What you can't bury give away
what you can't give away you must carry with you,
it is always heavier than you thought.

DIGGING

In this yard, barnyard
I dig with a shovel

beside the temple to the goddess
of open mouths: decayed
hay, steaming
in the humid sunlight, odour
of mildewed cardboard,

filling a box with rotted dung
to feed the melons.

I dig because I hold grudges
I dig with anger
I dig because I am hungry,
the dungpile scintillates with flies.

I try to ignore my sour clothes,
the murky bread devoured
at those breakfasts, drinking orange
and black acid, butter
tasting of silt, refrigerators,
old remorse

I defend myself with the past
which is not mine,
the archeology of manure:
this is not history, nothing ever
happened here, there were no battles

or victories: only deaths.
Witness this stained bone: pelvis
of some rodent, thrown or dragged here,
small, ferocious when cornered:

this bone is its last brittle scream,
the strict dogma of teeth.

I will wear it on a chain
around my neck: an amulet
to ward off anything

that is not a fact,
that is not food, including
symbols, monuments,
forgiveness, treaties, love.

TRICKS WITH MIRRORS

i

It's no coincidence
this is a used
furniture warehouse.

I enter with you
and become a mirror.

Mirrors
are the perfect lovers,

that's it, carry me up the stairs
by the edges, don't drop me,

that would be bad luck,
throw me on the bed

reflecting side up,
fall into me,

it will be your own
mouth you hit, firm and glassy,

your own eyes you find you
are up against   closed   closed

ii

There is more to a mirror
than you looking at

your full-length body
flawless but reversed,

there is more than this dead blue
oblong eye turned outwards to you.

Think about the frame.
The frame is carved, it is important,

it exists, it does not reflect you,
it does not recede and recede, it has limits

and reflections of its own.
There's a nail in the back

to hang it with; there are several nails,
think about the nails,

pay attention to the nail
marks in the wood,

they are important too.

iii

Don't assume it is passive
or easy, this clarity

with which I give you yourself.
Consider what restraint it

takes: breath withheld, no anger
or joy disturbing the surface

of the ice.
You are suspended in me

beautiful and frozen, I
preserve you, in me you are safe.

It is not a trick either,
it is a craft:

mirrors are crafty.

iv

I wanted to stop this,
this life flattened against the wall,

mute and devoid of colour,
built of pure light,

this life of vision only, split
and remote, a lucid impasse.

I confess: this is not a mirror,
it is a door

I am trapped behind.
I wanted you to see me here,

say the releasing word, whatever
that may be, open the wall.

Instead you stand in front of me
combing your hair.

v

You don't like these metaphors.
All right:

Perhaps I am not a mirror.
Perhaps I am a pool.

Think about pools.

YOU ARE HAPPY

The water turns
a long way down over the raw stone,
ice crusts around it

We walk separately
along the hill to the open
beach, unused
picnic tables, wind
shoving the brown waves, erosion, gravel
rasping on gravel.

In the ditch a deer
carcass, no head. Bird
running across the glaring
road against the low pink sun.

When you are this
cold you can think about
nothing but the cold, the images

hitting into your eyes
like needles, crystals, you are happy.

Songs of the Transformed

PIG SONG

This is what you changed me to:
a greypink vegetable with slug
eyes, buttock
incarnate, spreading like a slow turnip,

a skin you stuff so you may feed
in your turn, a stinking wart
of flesh, a large tuber
of blood which munches
and bloats. Very well then. Meanwhile

I have the sky, which is only half
caged, I have my weed corners,
I keep myself busy, singing
my song of roots and noses,

my song of dung. Madame,
this song offends you, these grunts
which you find oppressively sexual,
mistaking simple greed for lust.

I am yours. If you feed me garbage,
I will sing a song of garbage.
This is a hymn.

BULL SONG

For me there was no audience,
no brass music either,
only wet dust, the cheers
buzzing at me like flies,
like flies roaring.

I stood dizzied
with sun and anger,
neck muscle cut,
blood falling from the gouged shoulder.

Who brought me here
to fight against walls and blankets
and the gods with sinews of red and silver
who flutter and evade?

I turn, and my horns
gore blackness.
A mistake, to have shut myself
in this cask skin,
four legs thrust out like posts.
I should have remained grass.

The flies rise and settle.
I exit, dragged, a bale
of lump flesh.
The gods are awarded
the useless parts of my body.

For them this finish,
this death of mine is a game:
not the fact or act
but the grace with which they disguise it
justifies them.

RAT SONG

When you hear me singing
you get the rifle down
and the flashlight, aiming for my brain,
but you always miss

and when you set out the poison
I piss on it
to warn the others.

You think: *That one's too clever,
she's dangerous*, because
I don't stick around to be slaughtered
and you think I'm ugly too
despite my fur and pretty teeth
and my six nipples and snake tail.
All I want is love, you stupid
humanist. See if you can.

Right, I'm a parasite, I live off your
leavings, gristle and rancid fat,
I take without asking
and make nests in your cupboards
out of your suits and underwear.
You'd do the same if you could,

if you could afford to share
my crystal hatreds.
It's your throat I want, my mate
trapped in your throat.
Though you try to drown him
with your greasy person voice,
he is hiding / between your syllables
I can hear him singing.

CROW SONG

In the arid sun, over the field
where the corn has rotted and then
dried up, you flock and squabble.
Not much here for you, my people,
but there would be
if
if

In my austere black uniform
I raised the banner
which decreed *Hope*
and which did not succeed
and which is not allowed.
Now I must confront the angel
who says Win,
who tells me to wave any banner
that you will follow

for you ignore me, my
baffled people, you have been through
too many theories
too many stray bullets
your eyes are gravel, skeptical,

in this hard field
you pay attention only
to the rhetoric of seed
fruit stomach elbow.

You have too many leaders
you have too many wars,
all of them pompous and small,

you resist only when you feel
like dressing up,
you forget the sane corpses. . .

I know you would like a god
to come down and feed you
and punish you. That overcoat
on sticks is not alive
                              there are no angels
but the angels of hunger,
prehensile and soft as gullets
                              Watching you
my people, I become cynical,
you have defrauded me of hope
and left me alone with politics. . .

SONG OF THE WORMS

We have been underground too long,
we have done our work,
we are many and one,
we remember when we were human

We have lived among roots and stones,
we have sung but no one has listened,
we come into the open air
at night only to love

which disgusts the soles of boots,
their leather strict religion.

We know what a boot looks like
when seen from underneath,
we know the philosophy of boots,
their metaphysic of kicks and ladders.
We are afraid of boots
but contemptuous of the foot that needs them.

Soon we will invade like weeds,
everywhere but slowly;
the captive plants will rebel
with us, fences will topple,
brick walls ripple and fall,

there will be no more boots.
Meanwhile we eat dirt
and sleep; we are waiting
under your feet.
                When we say Attack
you will hear nothing
at first.

OWL SONG

I am the heart of a murdered woman
who took the wrong way home
who was strangled in a vacant lot and not buried
who was shot with care beneath a tree
who was mutilated by a crisp knife.
There are many of us.

I grew feathers and tore my way out of her;
I am shaped like a feathered heart.
My mouth is a chisel, my hands
the crimes done by hands.

I sit in the forest talking of death
which is monotonous:
though there are many ways of dying
there is only one death song,
the colour of mist:
it says Why Why

I do not want revenge, I do not want expiation,
I only want to ask someone
how I was lost,
how I was lost

I am the lost heart of a murderer
who has not yet killed,
who does not yet know he wishes
to kill; who is still the same
as the others

I am looking for him,
he will have answers for me,

he will watch his step, he will be
cautious and violent, my claws
will grow through his hands
and become claws, he will not be caught.

SIREN SONG

This is the one song everyone
would like to learn: the song
that is irresistible:

the song that forces men
to leap overboard in squadrons
even though they see the beached skulls

the song nobody knows
because anyone who has heard it
is dead, and the others can't remember.

Shall I tell you the secret
and if I do, will you get me
out of this bird suit?

I don't enjoy it here
squatting on this island
looking picturesque and mythical

with these two feathery maniacs,
I don't enjoy singing
this trio, fatal and valuable.

I will tell the secret to you,
to you, only to you.
Come closer. This song

is a cry for help: Help me!
Only you, only you can,
you are unique

at last. Alas
it is a boring song
but it works every time.

SONG OF THE FOX

Dear man with the accurate mafia
eyes and dog sidekicks, I'm tired of you,
the chase is no longer fun,
the dispute for this territory
of fences and hidden caverns
will never be won, let's
leave each other alone.

I saw you as another god
I could play with in this
maze of leaves and lovely blood,
performing hieroglyphs for you
with my teeth and agile feet
and dead hens harmless and jolly
as corpses in a detective story

but you were serious,
you wore gloves and plodded,
you saw me as vermin,
a crook in a fur visor;
the fate you aim at me
is not light literature.

O you misunderstand,
a game is not a law,
this dance is not a whim,
this kill is not a rival.
I crackle through your pastures,
I make no profit / like the sun
I burn and burn, this tongue
licks through your body also

SONG OF THE HEN'S HEAD

After the abrupt collision
with the blade, the Word,
I rest on the wood
block, my eyes
drawn back into their blue transparent
shells like molluscs;
I contemplate the Word

while the rest of me
which was never much under
my control, which was always

inarticulate, still runs
at random through the grass, a plea
for mercy, a single
flopping breast,

muttering about life
in its thickening red voice.

Feet and hands chase it, scavengers
intent on rape:
they want its treasures,
its warm rhizomes, enticing sausages,
its yellow grapes, its flesh
caves, five pounds of sweet money,
its juice and jellied tendons.
It tries to escape,
gasping through the neck, frantic.

They are welcome to it,

I contemplate the Word,
I am dispensable and peaceful.

The Word is an O,
outcry of the useless head,
pure space, empty and drastic,
the last word I said.
The word is No.

CORPSE SONG

I enter your night
like a darkened boat, a smuggler

These lanterns, my eyes
and heart are out

I bring you something
you do not want:

news of the country
I am trapped in,

news of your future:
soon you will have no voice

      (I resent your skin, I resent
       your lungs, your glib assumptions

Therefore sing now
while you have the choice

      (My body turned against me
       too soon, it was not a tragedy

      (I did not become
       a tree or a constellation

      (I became a winter coat the children
       thought they saw on the street corner

      (I became this illusion,
       this trick of ventriloquism

this blind noun, this bandage
crumpled at your dream's edge

or you will drift as I do
from head to head

swollen with words you never said,
swollen with hoarded love.

I exist in two places,
here and where you are.

Pray for me
not as I am but as I am.

Circe/Mud Poems

Through this forest
burned and sparse, the tines
of blunted trunks, charred branches

this forest of spines, antlers
the boat glides as if there is water

Red fireweed splatters the air
it is power, power
impinging, breaking over the seared rocks
in a slow collapse of petals

You move within range of my words
you land on the dry shore

You find what there is.

Men with the heads of eagles
no longer interest me
or pig-men, or those who can fly
with the aid of wax and feathers

or those who take off their clothes
to reveal other clothes
or those with skins of blue leather

or those golden and flat as a coat of arms
or those with claws, the stuffed ones
with glass eyes; or those
hierarchic as greaves and steam-engines.

All these I could create, manufacture,
or find easily: they swoop and thunder
around this island, common as flies,
sparks flashing, bumping into each other,

on hot days you can watch them
as they melt, come apart,
fall into the ocean
like sick gulls, dethronements, plane crashes.

I search instead for the others,
the ones left over,
the ones who have escaped from these
mythologies with barely their lives;
they have real faces and hands, they think
                              of themselves as
wrong somehow, they would rather be trees.

It was not my fault, these animals
who once were lovers

it was not my fault, the snouts
and hooves, the tongues
thickening and rough, the mouths grown over
with teeth and fur

I did not add the shaggy
rugs, the tusked masks,
they happened

I did not say anything, I sat
and watched, they happened
because I did not say anything.

It was not my fault, these animals
who could no longer touch me
through the rinds of their hardening skins,
these animals dying
of thirst because they could not speak

these drying skeletons
that have crashed and litter the ground
under the cliffs, these
wrecked words.

People come from all over to consult me, bringing their limbs
which have unaccountably fallen off, they don't know why,
my front porch is waist deep in hands, bringing their blood
hoarded in pickle jars, bringing their fears about their hearts,
which they either can or can't hear at night. They offer me
their pain, hoping in return for a word, a word, any word
from those they have assaulted daily, with shovels, axes,
electric saws, the silent ones, the ones they accused of being
silent because they would not speak in the received language.

I spend my days with my head pressed to the earth, to stones,
to shrubs, collecting the few muted syllables left over; in the
evenings I dispense them, a letter at a time, trying to be fair,
to the clamouring suppliants, who have built elaborate stair-
cases across the level ground so they can approach me on
their knees. Around me everything is worn down, the grass,
the roots, the soil, nothing is left but the bared rock.

Come away with me, he said, we will live on a desert island.
I said, I am a desert island. It was not what he had in mind.

I made no choice
I decided nothing

One day you simply appeared in your stupid boat,
your killer's hands, your disjointed body, jagged
   as a shipwreck,
skinny-ribbed, blue-eyed, scorched, thirsty, the usual,
pretending to be — what?   a survivor?

Those who say they want nothing
want everything.
It was not this greed
that offended me, it was the lies.

Nevertheless I gave you
the food you demanded for the journey
you said you planned; but you planned no journey
and we both knew it.

You've forgotten that,
you made the right decision.
The trees bend in the wind, you eat, you rest,
you think of nothing,
your mind, you say,
is like your hands, vacant:

vacant is not innocent.

There must be more for you to do
than permit yourself to be shoved
by the wind from coast
to coast to coast, boot on the boat prow
to hold the wooden body
under, soul in control

Ask at my temples
where the moon snakes, tongues of the dark
speak like bones unlocking, leaves falling
of a future you won't believe in

Ask who keeps the wind
Ask what is sacred

Don't you get tired of killing
those whose deaths have been predicted
and are therefore dead already?

Don't you get tired of wanting
to live forever?

Don't you get tired of saying Onward?

You may wonder why I'm not describing the landscape for you. This island with its complement of scrubby trees, picturesque bedrock, ample weather and sunsets, lavish white sand beaches and so on. (For which I am not responsible.) There are travel brochures that do this better, and in addition they contain several very shiny illustrations so real you can almost touch the ennui of actually being here. They leave out the insects and the castaway bottles but so would I in their place; all advertisements are slanted, including this one.

You had a chance to read up on the place before you came: even allowing for the distortion, you knew what you were getting into. And you weren't invited, just lured.

But why should I make excuses? Why should I describe the landscape for you? You live here, don't you? Right now I mean. See for yourself.

You stand at the door
bright as an icon,

dressed in your thorax,
the forms of the indented
ribs and soft belly underneath
carved into the slick bronze
so that it fits you almost
like a real skin

You are impervious
with hope, it hardens you,
this joy, this expectation, gleams
in your hands like axes

If I allow you what you say
you want, even the day after

this, will you hurt me?

If you do I will fear you,
If you don't I will despise you

To be feared, to be despised,
these are your choices.

There are so many things I want
you to have. This is mine, this
tree, I give you its name,

here is food, white like roots, red,
growing in the marsh, on the shore,
I pronounce these names for you also.

This is mine, this island, you can have
the rocks, the plants
that spread themselves flat over
the thin soil, I renounce them.

You can have this water,
this flesh, I abdicate,

I watch you, you claim
without noticing it,
you know how to take.

Holding my arms down
holding my head down by the hair

mouth gouging my face
and neck, fingers groping into my flesh

      (Let go, this is extortion,
         you force my body to confess
         too fast and
         incompletely, its words
         tongueless and broken)

If I stopped believing you
this would be hate

Why do you need this?
What do you want me to admit?

My face, my other faces
stretching over it like
rubber, like flowers opening
and closing, like rubber,
like liquid steel,
like steel. Face of steel.

Look at me and see your reflection.

The fist, withered and strung
on a chain around my neck
wishes to hold on
to me, commands
your transformation

The dead fingers mutter
against each other, thumbs rubbing
the worn moon rituals

but you are protected,
you do not snarl,
you do not change,

in the hard slot of your mouth
your teeth remain fixed,
zippered to a silver curve;
nothing rusts.

Through two holes in the leather
the discs of your eyes gleam
white as dulled quartz;
you wait

the fist stutters, gives up,
you are not visible

You unbuckle the fingers of the fist,
you order me to trust you.

This is not something that can be renounced,
it must renounce.

It lets go of me
and I open like a hand
cut off at the wrist

(It is the
arm feels pain

But the severed hand
the hand clutches at freedom)

Last year I abstained
this year I devour

without guilt
which is also an art

Your flawed body, sickle
scars on the chest, moonmarks, the botched knee
that nevertheless bends when you will it to

Your body, broken and put together
not perfectly, marred
by war but moving
despite that with such ease and leisure

Your body that includes everything
you have done, you have had done
to you and goes beyond it

This is not what I want
but I want this also.

This story was told to me by another traveller, just passing through. It took place in a foreign country, as everything does.

When he was young he and another boy constructed a woman out of mud. She began at the neck and ended at the knees and elbows: they stuck to the essentials. Every sunny day they would row across to the island where she lived, in the afternoon when the sun had warmed her, and make love to her, sinking with ecstacy into her soft moist belly, her brown wormy flesh where small weeds had already rooted. They would take turns, they were not jealous, she preferred them both. Afterwards they would repair her, making her hips more spacious, enlarging her breasts with their shining stone nipples.

His love for her was perfect, he could say anything to her, into her he spilled his entire life. She was swept away in a sudden flood. He said no woman since then has equalled her.

Is this what you would like me to be, this mud woman? Is this what I would like to be? It would be so simple.

We walk in the cedar groves
intending love, no one is here

but the suicides, returned
in the shapes of birds
with their razor-blue
feathers, their beaks like stabs, their eyes
red as the food of the dead, their single
iridescent note,
complaint or warning:

Everything dies, they say,
Everything dies.
Their colours pierce the branches.

Ignore them. Lie on the ground
like this, like the season
which is full and not theirs;

our bodies hurt them,
our mouths tasting of pears, grease,
onions, earth we eat
which was not enough for them,
the pulse under the skin, their eyes
radiate anger, they are thirsty:

Die, they whisper, Die,
their eyes consuming
themselves like stars, impersonal:

they do not care whose
blood fills the sharp trenches
where they were buried, stake through
the heart; as long
as there is blood.

Not you I fear but that other
who can walk through flesh,
queen of the two dimensions.

She wears a necklace of small teeth,
she knows the ritual, she gets results,
she wants it to be like this:

Don't stand there
with your offerings of dead sheep,
chunks of wood, young children, blood,

your wet eyes, your body
gentle and taut with love,
assuming I can do nothing about it

but accept, accept, accept.
I'm not the sea, I'm not pure blue,
I don't have to take

anything you throw into me.
I close myself over, deaf as an eye,
deaf as a wound, which listens

to nothing but its own pain:
Get out of here.
Get out of here.

You think you are safe at last. After your misadventures, lies, losses and cunning departures, you are doing what most veterans would like to do: you are writing a travel book. In the seclusion of this medium-sized brick building, which is ancient though not sacred any more, you disappear every morning into your white plot, filling in the dangers as you go: those with the sinister flowers who tempted you to forsake pain, the perilous and hairy eye of the groin you were forced to blind, the ones you mistook for friends, those eaters of human flesh. You add details, you colour the dead red.

I bring you things on trays, food mostly, an ear, a finger. You trust me so you are no longer cautious, you abandon yourself to your memoranda, you traverse again those menacing oceans; in the clutch of your story, your disease, you are helpless.

But it is not finished, that saga. The fresh monsters are already breeding in my head. I try to warn you, though I know you will not listen.

So much for art. So much for prophecy.

When you look at nothing
what are you looking at?
Whose face floats on the water
dissolving like a paper plate?

It's the first one, remember,
the one you thought you abandoned
along with the furniture.

You returned to her after the other war
and look what happened.
Now you are wondering
whether to do it again.

Meanwhile she sits in her chair
waxing and waning
like an inner tube or a mother,
breathing out, breathing in,

surrounded by bowls, bowls, bowls,
tributes from the suitors
who are having a good time in the kitchen

waiting for her to decide
on the dialogue for this evening
which will be in perfect taste
and will include tea and sex
dispensed graciously both at once.

She's up to something, she's weaving
histories, they are never right,
she has to do them over,
she is weaving her version,

the one you will believe in,
the only one you will hear.

Here are the holy birds,
grub white, with solid blood
wobbling on their heads and throats

They eat seeds and dirt, live in a shack,
lay eggs, each bursting
with a yellow sun, divine
as lunch, squeeze out,
there is only one word for it, shit,
which transforms itself to beets
or peonies, if you prefer.

We too eat
and grow fat, you aren't content
with that, you want more,
you want me to tell you
the future. That's my job,
one of them, but I advise you
don't push your luck.

To know the future
there must be a death.
Hand me the axe.

As you can see
the future is a mess,
snarled guts all over the yard
and that snakey orange eye
staring up from the sticky grass
round as a target, stopped
dead, intense as love.

Now it is winter.
By winter I mean: white, silent,
hard, you didn't expect that,

it isn't supposed to occur
on this kind of island,
and it never has before

but I am the place where
all desires are fulfilled,
I mean: all desires.

Is it too cold for you?
This is what you requested,
this ice, this crystal

wall, this puzzle. You solve it.

It's the story that counts. No use telling me this isn't a story, or not the same story. I know you've fulfilled everything you promised, you love me, we sleep till noon and we spend the rest of the day eating, the food is superb, I don't deny that. But I worry about the future. In the story the boat disappears one day over the horizon, just disappears, and it doesn't say what happens then. On the island that is. It's the animals I'm afraid of, they weren't part of the bargain, in fact you didn't mention them, they may transform themselves back into men. Am I really immortal, does the sun care, when you leave will you give me back the words? Don't evade, don't pretend you won't leave after all: you leave in the story and the story is ruthless.

There are two islands
at least, they do not exclude each other

On the first I am right,
the events run themselves through
almost without us,

we are open, we are closed,
we express joy, we proceed
as usual, we watch for
omens, we are sad

and so forth, it is over,
I am right, it starts again,
jerkier this time and faster,

I could say it without looking, the animals,
the blackened trees, the arrivals,

the bodies, words, it goes and goes,
I could recite it backwards.

The second I know nothing about
because it has never happened;

this land is not finished,
this body is not reversible.

We walk through a field, it is November,

the grass is yellow, tinged
with grey, the apples

are still on the trees,
they are orange, astonishing, we are standing

in a clump of weeds near the dead elms
our faces upturned, the wet flakes
falling onto our skin and melting

We lick the melted snow
from each other's mouths,
we see birds, four of them, they are gone, and

a stream, not frozen yet, in the mud
beside it the track of a deer

IS / NOT

i

Love is not a profession
genteel or otherwise

sex is not dentistry
the slick filling of aches and cavities

you are not my doctor
you are not my cure,

nobody has that
power, you are merely a fellow/traveller.

Give up this medical concern,
buttoned, attentive,

permit yourself anger
and permit me mine

which needs neither
your approval nor your surprise

which does not need to be made legal
which is not against a disease

but against you,
which does not need to be understood

or washed or cauterized,
which needs instead

to be said and said.
Permit me the present tense.

ii

I am not a saint or a cripple,
I am not a wound; now I will see
whether I am a coward.

I dispose of my good manners,
you don't have to kiss my wrists.

This is a journey, not a war,
there is no outcome,
I renounce predictions

and aspirins, I resign the future
as I would resign an expired passport:
picture and signature are gone
along with holidays and safe returns.

We're stuck here
on this side of the border
in this country of thumbed streets and stale buildings

where there is nothing spectacular
to see and the weather is ordinary

where *love* occurs in its pure form only
on the cheaper of the souvenirs

where we must walk slowly,
where we may not get anywhere

or anything, where we keep going,
fighting our ways, our way
not out but through.

EATING FIRE

i

Eating fire

is your ambition:
to swallow the flame down
take it into your mouth
and shoot it forth, a shout or an incandescent
tongue, a word
exploding from you in gold, crimson,
unrolling in a brilliant scroll

To be lit up from within
vein by vein

To be the sun

(Taught by a sideshow man)

ii

Dead man by the roadside
thrown from the overturning
truck or hit by something, a car, a bullet

On his head the hair glows,
the blood inside ignited,
short blue thorns of flame still flickering over him

Was it worth it?   ask him.
(Did you save anyone?)

He gets up and walks away, the fire
growing on him like fur

iii

Here the children have a custom. After the celebration of
evil they take those vacant heads that shone once with such
anguish and glee and throw them over the bridge, watching
the smash, orange, as they hit below. We were standing
underneath when you told it. People do that with them-
selves when they are finished, light scooped out. He landed
here, you said, marking it with your foot.

You wouldn't do it that way, empty, you wouldn't wait,
you would jump with the light still in you.

iv

This is your trick or miracle,
to be consumed and rise
intact, over and over, even for myths there is
a limit, the time when you accomplish
failure and return
from the fire minus your skin.

The new eyes are golden and
maniac, a bird's or lion's

Through them you see
everything, as you wished,
each object (lake, tree, woman)

transfigured with your love, shining
in its life, its pain, like waves, tears, ice,
like flesh laid open to the bone.

v

To be the sun, moving through space

distant and indifferent, giving
light of a kind for those watching

To learn how to
live this way. or not. to choose

to be also human, the body
mortal and faded, incapable of saving

itself, praying
as it falls. in its own way.

FOUR AUGURIES

i

Walking by lakeshore, feet in slush, it rains,
no grace you'd say in the dirty
ice or the goose-turd-coloured grass.

Traffic back there, illegible, passive
metal stuffed with muggy life.

Near the fence a fat man with binoculars
waddles backwards, feeding store bread
to a herd of acquiescent birds.

Bathhouse, walls patchy and scribbled over,
unredeemed, stagnant in this winter.

ii

Though your body stowed in its heavy coat
is still a body: the sleeves promise me

arms, the pockets let loose their hands,
the lines on this hand hide a future

I decode only by the sense
of touch, light and urgent

the blind must rely on

iii

Gulls on the breakwater, thin sounds against
the shale-grey lake. Part of us, distinct

from us, *This* , we say, taking
wet skin, smell of wet cloth, specifies,

I gather you, ear, collar, tuft of damp hair,
creases in your suddenly unfolding face

You are more than I wanted,
this is new, this greed for the real.

iv

Nothing we planned
or have understood this far. No words,
no shelter

          Out here
in the open, the sky has released an owl
which drifts down and pauses

now, feathers warm snow,
hooked claws gripping the branch.

With its hooded predator's
eyes it blesses us:

                    mouth against throat

Omen: soft hunter

HEAD AGAINST WHITE

i

Swift curve of the lip, nose, forehead,
thrust of the bristling
jaw: a military stance.

Face closed, teeth and eyes concealed,
the body sheeted / muscles frozen shut.

Be alive, my hands
plead with you, *Be alive*.

Scar on the chin, allusion
to a minor incident, oval

dent in the skull
my fingers return to, mention with touch, cherish
as though the wound is my own.

ii

The way your face
unhinges and comes apart:

confident upturned mouth, eyes
crouched in the sockets, maimed and lightblue with terror,

man on a roof's edge balancing
the moment before he topples, no can't
move, regain ground, under your weight the floor

peels back, recedes, leaving you
alone in the silent air.

It's all right. This magic fails.

No use to be the sky,
bending and watching.

iii

Those times we have rumours of, arctic or alpine
when the wind and snow have stopped
at last and the rescue teams
with their tools and joyous motors

are out chasing the survivors
back from their cold refuge, hermitage
of ice to the land of sharp
colours and enforced life

Surely this is the first sign they find:
this face, rigid and fierce
with renunciation, floating up through
                              the softening white rock
like a carved long-buried god,

revealed word

iv

Under the skin's fixed surface: destroyed face
caving in on itself

No way I can walk back with you
to the country of these mutilations.

You lie here, safe, cared for, casualty
of a war that took place elsewhere,

your body replaying for you
the deserts, jungles, the smell of rotting

leaves, harsh acid scent of blood,
the mistakes, the intersections,

fact with fact, accidents
that perhaps never occurred.

Break it, I tell you, *Break
it*. Geology wins. The layer

of trite histories presses you down,
monotony of stone. Oval frame.

v

In the mirror, face to glass face,
noon, the winter light strikes

through the window, your eyes flare, the city
burns whitely behind us. Blood flows
under the molten skin.

To move beyond the mirror's edge, discard
these scars, medals, to pronounce

your own flesh. Now

                    to be this
man on fire, hands open and held
out, not empty, giving

time / From these hardened
hours, these veteran
faces, burials

to rise up living

THERE IS ONLY ONE OF EVERYTHING

Not a tree but the tree
we saw, it will never exist, split by the wind
                    and bending down
like that again. What will push out of the earth

later, making it summer, will not be
grass, leaves, repetition, there will
have to be other words. When my

eyes close language vanishes. The cat
with the divided face, half black half orange
nests in my scruffy fur coat, I drink tea,

fingers curved around the cup, impossible
to duplicate these flavours. The table
and freak plates glow softly, consuming themselves,

I look out at you and you occur
in this winter kitchen, random as trees or sentences,
entering me, fading like them, in time you will disappear

but the way you dance by yourself
on the tile floor to a worn song, flat and mournful,
so delighted, spoon waved in one hand, wisps of
                    roughened hair

sticking up from your head, it's your surprised
body, pleasure I like. I can even say it,
though only once and it won't

last: I want this. I want
this.

LATE AUGUST

This is the plum season, the nights
blue and distended, the moon
hazed, this is the season of peaches

with their lush lobed bulbs
that glow in the dusk, apples
that drop and rot
sweetly, their brown skins veined as glands

No more the shrill voices
that cried *Need Need*
from the cold pond, bladed
and urgent as new grass

Now it is the crickets
that say *Ripe Ripe*
slurred in the darkness, while the plums

dripping on the lawn outside
our window, burst
with a sound like thick syrup
muffled and slow

The air is still
warm, flesh moves over
flesh, there is no

hurry

i

Book of Ancestors: these brutal, with curled
beards and bulls' heads . these flattened,
slender with ritual . these contorted
by ecstacy or pain . these bearing
knife, leaf, snake

and these, closer to us,
copper hawkman arched on the squat rock
pyramid, the plumed and beak-
nosed priests pressing his arms and feet
down, heart slashed from his opened
flesh, lifted to where
the sun, red and dilated
with his blood, glows in the still hungry sky

Whether he thinks this is
an act of will:

the life set free
by him alone, offered, ribs expanding
by themselves, bone petals,
the heart released and flickering in the
taloned hand, handful of liquid
fire joined to that other fire
an instant before the sacrificed eyes
burst like feathered stars in the darkness

of the painted border.

ii

So much for the gods and their
static demands . our demands, former
demands, death patterns
obscure as fragments of an
archeology, these frescoes
on a crumbling temple
wall we look at now and can scarcely
piece together

        History
is over, we take place
in a season, an undivided
space, no necessities

hold us closed, distort
us. I lean behind you, mouth touching
your spine, my arms around
you, palm above the heart,
your blood insistent under
my hand, quick and mortal

iii

Midwinter, the window
is luminous with blown snow, the fire
burns inside its bars

On the floor your body curves
like that: the ancient pose, neck slackened, arms
thrown above the head, vital
throat and belly lying
undefended. light slides over you,
this is not an altar, they are not
acting or watching

You are intact, you turn
towards me, your eyes opening, the eyes
intricate and easily bruised, you open

yourself to me gently, what
they tried, we
tried but could never do
before . without blood, the killed
heart . to take
that risk, to offer life and remain

alive, open yourself like this and become whole